SCM PAPERBACKS

now published

MEN OF UNITY *by Stephen Neill*
THE MIND OF JESUS *by William Barclay*
CRUCIFIED AND CROWNED *by William Barclay*
JESUS AS THEY SAW HIM *by William Barclay*
ST PAUL AND THE GOSPEL OF JESUS *by Charles E. Raven*
THE BIBLE IN THE AGE OF SCIENCE *by Alan Richardson*
INTRODUCING THE CHRISTIAN FAITH *by A. M. Ramsey,
Archbishop of Canterbury*
THE BRITISH CHURCHES TODAY *by Kenneth Slack*
CHRISTIAN DEVIATIONS: THE CHALLENGE OF THE SECTS
by Horton Davies
DESPATCH FROM NEW DELHI *by Kenneth Slack*
NEW DELHI SPEAKS: *World Council of Churches*
GOD'S CROSS IN OUR WORLD *by David L. Edwards*
LOOKING AT THE VATICAN COUNCIL *by Bernard Pawley*
BEGINNING THE OLD TESTAMENT *by Erik Routley*
CHRISTIAN FAITH AND LIFE *by William Temple*

future titles will include

HONEST TO GOD *by John A. T. Robinson*
WE THE PEOPLE *by Kathleen Bliss*
THE GOSPELS *by William Barclay*
CHRISTIANS AND THE HOME *by Ruth Adam*

books which everyone can learn from and keep

WILLIAM TEMPLE

Christian Faith and Life

SCM PRESS LTD
BLOOMSBURY STREET LONDON

also by William Temple

ABOUT CHRIST

lectures to students in 1921 and 1925
reissued in 1962 with a preface by
the Archbishop of York
and an essay by J. Eric Fenn

FIRST PUBLISHED 1931
SIXTEEN REPRINTS 1931–1957
THIS EDITION 1963
© SCM PRESS LTD 1963
PRINTED IN THE NETHERLANDS
BY DRUKKERIJ HOLLAND N.V. AMSTERDAM

CONTENTS

O THOU who art the Light of the minds that know Thee, the Life of the souls that love Thee, and the Strength of the wills that serve Thee, help us so to know Thee that we may truly love Thee, so to love Thee that we may fully serve Thee, whom to serve is perfect freedom; through Jesus Christ our Lord.

FOREWORD (1963)
by F. R. Barry, Bishop of Southwell

'LAST time I saw you,' said the Headmaster of a Grammar School in Uganda to me in February 1962, 'it was in the University Church at Oxford, during Archbishop Temple's mission.' That was thirty-one years ago and its creative influence still persists.

This book, which contains the addresses given then, has already run through seventeen impressions, and there is now a demand for another edition. Indeed it is something of a Christian classic. For although in some respects it is dated—it reflects the period out of which it came—there is about it a certain timeless quality which enables it to speak to the condition of religious seekers in greatly changed circumstances and a very different climate of opinion.

These addresses were given in a situation—political, social and intellectual—which the university world to-day can neither remember nor easily imagine—pre-war, pre-social revolution, pre-Ayer, pre-Tillich and pre-Bultmann. They could take the older 'Greats' course for granted and deploy philosophical argument on a wide front. No one had yet suggested that the concepts handled by metaphysics were 'meaningless.' The author himself refers to *Christus Veritas* for a fuller development of his line of thought. Nearly thirty years later another Archbishop of York taking another mission to Oxford began by saying that, at the outset, he did not intend to use the word God. 'That is because the word has become conventional, and I am asking you to think about a reality rather than a word.' [1] And it would indeed be an educational exercise to contrast the approaches of the two Archbishops, in reflecting the radically changed background against which their message was delivered. Temple's opening was '"In the beginning God." The Bible starts there.' Ramsey began: 'We live in a puzzling world. Each of us is also something of a puzzle to himself and to other people . . . I want to suggest that I am talking about what is already going on inside you and not about a sort of outside technicality which I have come to sell to you.' The pundits might call that 'existentialist,' and why should we grudge them their simple pleasures? My point is simply that the different start suggests the difference in the situation to which these two missions were addressed.

But the striking thing is that, in spite of that, both sets of addresses follow the same course and both say more or less the same thing—at times in virtually the same words. And, after all, how could it be otherwise? For both are concerned to preach Jesus Christ, who is 'yesterday and today the same and forever.'

In this there are far-reaching implications. After the bitter experience of the war Temple in later life fully realised that his earlier hope of a 'Christian world-view' was premature and possibly unattainable. He predicted that the theological emphasis would shift back as events

---

[1] A. M. Ramsey (now Archbishop of Canterbury), *Introducing the Christian Faith* (SCM Paperbacks, 1961).

were compelling it to shift, from the Incarnation to the original Gospel of deliverance from the powers of hell and death. He saw, moreover, that we have claimed too much, and perhaps built up a too ambitious structure of doctrinal and philosophical affirmation.

We must go back again to the foundations. Christianity, as we have received it, is built into an intellectual framework constructed in a pre-scientific age out of materials which the twentieth century finds it increasingly difficult to accept.

What has been its strength is now a primary obstacle in communicating it to the modern mind. For the twentieth century thinks in different terms, and what has hitherto guaranteed that Christianity should be embodied in contemporary thought and culture now seems to interpose a barrier. It looks as though the Church —all the churches—must be prepared for a radical reconstruction in the statement and presentation of its creed. Can it be translated from the traditional thought-forms into others more significant to our own day, without evacuating its real content? Would the picture in a new frame be the same picture or is the frame part of the composition? The question is as old as the Fourth Gospel, and the coming generations will have to answer it.

Christianity can never be 'demythologised' in so far as that means any attempt to separate it from the faith in the historical Jesus Christ and the facts on which that faith depends, for then it would just not be Christianity; it would have become a different religion. Fundamentally it can never change. And the popular demand that it should be 'modernised,' in the sense of eliminating its profundities and rubbing out of it all that is mysterious in order that it may thus be accommodated to the shallow mentality of ad-mass, is one that the Church cannot entertain without gross betrayal of its trust. Christianity must always be a 'scandal.'

Nevertheless, it *is* meant for all men. And the faith of Christians, what they have found in Christ, has from the beginning been presented in terms of myth, imagery and symbol drawn from semitic and hellenistic sources. These myths and symbols ring no bell in the twentieth-century mind, and, falsely interpreted as factual statements, they make the Christian religion seem incredible or, even if credible, irrelevant. Is it possible to find any other symbols through which to express the significance of Christ and His place in the destiny of men? Is it possible to present Christianity, the thing itself, as faith in God and man mediated through Jesus Christ in new and less mystifying categories? That, in my judgement, is one of the biggest questions before the Church during the next half-century. It may have to find its way to a new theology, formed out of the thought and experience of its own time, to interpret the world and man's place within it in the light revealed through the mind of Christ. It may even be that years hence a mission to Oxford will have to be presented in terms which neither Temple nor Ramsey would approve.

But what will be central will still be the same Person. For if one thing is certain it is that apart from Him Christianity can have nothing at all to say.

But it is time to return to William Temple. I am proud

to be asked to introduce this reprint, and it awakens many treasured memories. I was Vicar of St Mary's, Oxford, at the time and, accordingly, with my colleague Harry Baines, now Bishop of Wellington, New Zealand, who was then the SCM Secretary, had the main responsibility for the mission and the work of preparation that led up to it.

That week proved to be one of Temple's finest hours. He was asked to do something exceptionally difficult, and no other man in England could have done it. Each generation has its own needs. What was needed then and there was a demonstration.

In the disillusioned aftermath of the first war Oxford was going through a very bad patch—and so, probably, were the other universities. Religious and moral life was at a low ebb. College chapels were virtually empty. Christianity was almost a dirty word. Christian belief was commonly regarded as the refuge of the mentally second-rate—few, anyhow, were prepared to take it seriously.

The job of the University Church, in that context, was to get Christianity back upon the map—to exhibit its relevance to the life of Oxford and as something intellectually respectable. And precisely that Temple did so grandly. I still meet people in many parts of the world who say that it was that week in St Mary's which enabled them to hold on to their Christianity.

The appeal was not confined to undergraduates. One evening, I remember, the major part of the Balliol senior common room was present. The whole University was made aware that something highly significant was happening. It was indeed the turning of the tide in the religious life of the universities. The intellectual battle is not yet won. Do the Churches even now realise that if they fail at the university level they are almost bound, in the end, to fail everywhere? But at least it can be claimed that Christian thought is now respected in academic circles and that, by and large, there are in the universities higher percentages of professing Christians than almost anywhere else in the population.

That is largely due, under God, to the addresses which are now reprinted in this book.

It was not, of course, only the addresses. It was Temple himself and the quality of his spirit. There had not been a mission in Oxford since the war.

The novelty which made it sound exciting, and the eminence of the advertised missioner, brought reporters swarming into Oxford hoping to pick up stories of 'sensations.' Needless to say, they found nothing of the kind. What they found was a speaker in the pulpit speaking in quiet, unemotional tones to a vast congregation quietly absorbed. Nothing seemed to be happening at all! That was the way the Archbishop went to work. But of course it was not merely a mental exercise. There was very much more to it than that. Temple has been accused of 'emotional poverty,' and he always kept himself under strict control. But something passed from him to his hearers which may fairly be said to have taken possession of them. It is not possible now to recall the 'atmosphere' to anyone who was not there at the time. But one haunting, unforgettable moment may serve to convey to the reader some idea of it, when a thousand undergraduates were *whispering* 'love so amazing, so divine demands my soul, my life, my all.' (See page 89.)[1] But he knew that devotion, however deeply felt, must be translated into pedestrian practice if it is not to be positively enervating.

His final address dealt with little things which, if every committed Christian were to do them, would revolutionise corporate life. As he once said to another student audience: 'Whether you are setting out for the New Jerusalem or making tracks for the nearest café, in either case you have got to take the next step.'

The addresses were given, apparently, without notes; at most he had a half-sheet of note-paper. He must have thought a great deal about them, but so far as I know, they had never been written down. I asked him once how he managed to prepare his innumerable sermons and addresses. What he said was: 'When I book an engagement I spend a few minutes in thinking what line to take, and then I don't think about it any more. When I get to the church I find it has done itself.'

What a gift from the subconscious mind! It was, I believe, inherited from his father. It enabled him to do several things at once. For example, taking the chair at a committee he would be writing his letters most of the time and apparently taking very little notice. Then he would say, 'We should adjourn now,' and close with

1 This is told in Iremonger's *William Temple*, p. 378. I was in my stall at the time and I can vouch for it.

a masterly summing up of nearly everything that had been said.

It was fascinating to watch how that gift saved him from total exhaustion during that week. He stayed with us in our home in Holywell and naturally we did our best to take care of him. He used to be out nearly all day, engaged in interviews with enquirers, small group meetings and the like and, perhaps, piles of official correspondence, and came home in the evening already pretty tired.

We used to give him his dinner alone in my study, to secure him such quiet as we could before he had to deliver his address. How did he spend that hour?

To our astonishment, what he used to demand was a thriller which he read steadily till it was time for church. 'The important thing is,' he explained, 'to keep your mind *off* what you are going to do.' Then he went to St Mary's and straight into the pulpit, and spoke vitally, freshly and convincingly as though that had been his only task that day. It all came out in perfect prose sentences, almost exactly as it is printed here. I read the proofs of the *Church Times* reports for him, and scarcely ever had to correct a word. Those reports, again virtually unaltered, were then put together to make this book.

That account, from actual observation of how a great man's mind worked, may be interesting to readers who did not know him personally. But let it not be supposed that his power and influence were merely due to a fortunate trick of memory. Temple's moral and spiritual stature grew from the depths of a life hid with God. That was the abiding secret of his serenity. He never fussed and he never got rattled, even when the strain was near breaking-point. As it is written on his grave at Canterbury, *Thou shalt keep him in perfect peace, whose mind is stayed on Thee.*

I hope that this edition will initiate some new readers into a study of his creative mind.

RUSSELL SOUTHWELL

PREFACE

THE addresses here published were delivered on eight successive evenings in St Mary's Church, Oxford, in February 1931, during a Mission which I conducted there with the assistance of Canon T. W. Pym. They were delivered from very brief notes, and I am indebted to the *Church Times* for their permission to use their *verbatim* report for this volume. I have here and there edited them very slightly, but for the most part I have left the phrasing as it was, even when it was such as is appropriate only to the spoken, and not to the written, word.

It must be remembered that the effect of addresses given on such an occasion depends mainly on factors which cannot be reproduced: the preparation that has gone on in advance, the 'atmosphere,' the sense of fellowship in the congregation, and the personal reactions between the speaker and his hearers.

The order followed was not varied. After an opening hymn that prayer was said which follows this preface; then the Lord's Prayer; then came the first section of the address. This was followed by a hymn at the place marked in this volume by a row of asterisks. Then came the second part of the address, usually much shorter. At the close of this the congregation knelt while I read, with silent pauses for meditation, those passages of

Scripture which are here printed with each address, except that on the last evening the address was followed by a hymn, and I then used the prayer and benediction printed in that place.

I have included these quotations and that prayer in order to recall to those who were present as fully as possible the experience which we shared. But I cannot hope to convey it to others. For it was not of my making. It was due to the prayers offered both before and throughout that week in Oxford and elsewhere.

I will only add that, if anyone wishes to follow in more detail the general line of thought pursued in these addresses, he will find it worked out in my book, *Christus Veritas*.

WILLIAM EBOR

Bishopthorpe, York
February 24, 1931

1

WHAT DO WE MEAN BY 'GOD'?

'In the beginning God.' The Bible starts there. That is one difference between the old world and ours. In the old world practically everyone was convinced that there existed divine beings or one Divine being, and the only question asked was, What is the character of the Divine? It was certainly there, but what was it like? In the modern world we all agree about certain things that the word 'God' must mean; and the question now is whether any reality corresponds to the meaning. We should not now bestow the name of God on such figures as the Olympian gods of the Homeric poems. We might think of them as super-human in some respects, and perhaps *infra*-human in others. But it would never occur to us to say of any of them, 'He is God.' We might say, 'He is a god,' deliberately meaning by that something very different.

In fact, it has become quite impossible for us to believe in a multiplicity of gods. Our notion of God is of such a sort as to exclude the possibility of there being more than one. Christians do not say there is only one God, because they would really like to believe in several, but cannot press their demand quite so far. They mean that their conception of God is of such a kind that there can only be One; there can only be one Creator of the universe, there can be only one Being supreme over everything that exists. There can be only one Being who is Himself the consummation of all that we mean by good.

The word 'God' means the union of absolute goodness and absolute power. Does that union exist? Is it a reality? Now you will not expect me in one evening to give you any exhaustive answer to that question. I can only suggest lines for you to follow. But before we start on any of them, remember that so far as religion has any interest in this question, the interest would be destroyed if the reality of God could be proved in the sense in which mathematical propositions are proved. As soon as the reality of God was an intellectual certainty, there would no longer be any spiritual merit in faith. From the point of view of religion, not only of the Christian religion, faith is something nobler in its own kind than certainty. For us finite beings in this world that which most of all calls forth our noblest capacities into action is always a hazard of some kind, never a certainty. It is when we are ready to stake our lives on something being so, or to make something so that is not so, that nobility begins to appear in human nature.

To adapt our lives with careful caution to fully established certainties is not in the least noble or heroic: it is merely sensible. It is good to be sensible; it is better to be heroic; but it is best of all to be both, although very few of us are. The whole case of religion, through all ages, is that it is a venture, a quest of faith; and it has ennobled men for that reason. There may be no difficulty in staking one's life on an ideal because it is splendid, even if the possibility of its attainment is extremely remote; but here we are not so much staking our lives on an ideal we may be able to realise, but rather on beliefs which must, in themselves, be either true or false.

It would be a contradiction of what religious people mean by God if we were to begin thinking of it as what is going to happen some day. Faith in God is faith in an ever-present, all-sustaining Power. There are paradoxes enough about it, but that is its note, and if you take that out of it, the distinctive power which it exercises over men's lives is at once gone. By what kind of process of thought are we to approach the solution of such a question?

There used in this University to be a study called 'Mods' (or formal) logic, which divided the processes by which men think when in pursuit of truth into deductive and inductive. If God exists, you may draw deductions from His nature, but from the very nature of deduction itself you cannot reach Him by means of it. Nor can you hope to get there by induction, by looking about in the world for a great variety of events which you cannot explain in any other way. You could never be sure that there was one cause which explained them all; you would therefore never reach God.

Moreover, we know quite well that as soon as anyone points to coincidences as evidence of apparent design in the life of nature, others are encountered which tell just the other way. Design must be to an end; the end we think of as human welfare, and our forefathers used to argue that the tendency of natural arrangements to conduce so much to human welfare was evidence for the Being of God. But the more that we discover about the processes of nature the more that evidence becomes at least as doubtful as it is convincing. Our method must be critical and systematic. Is there, in our experience, any entity or principle which is, whenever it is applicable, a source of ultimate explanation about which no further question arises? If there is, it will then be in accordance with the most rational possible method that we should make the hypothesis that this principle is the explanation of the universe. If anything is to explain the universe it must be something which raises no further questions. Throughout the whole realm of scientific inquiry you ask the question Why? and to the answer you ask Why? again, and that is how science goes on. It now gives us a universe which was once very, very hot, and is going to be some day very cold; how it got there or how it became hot it cannot explain. In other words, the mysterious universe presented to you by such great astronomers as Sir James Jeans is just a brute fact. Take any part of it and it is explicable by its relation to the other parts. Taken in its entirety, it explains nothing, and nothing explains it.

But it is the fact that in our very limited experience, whenever we can trace anything that we observe to the action of intelligent purpose, we are in fact satisfied. There is a stock illustration, and I do not know any better, so I will use it once again. You may be studying the geological formation of rocks in a hilly district. You come across there odd formations of the rock and stone; among others there is one that puzzles you particularly, because it consists of little heaps in a straight line across the crest of the hill. The former you account for by scientific means; you reconstruct the past actions and reactions which have gone on in accordance with known laws; you go on to ask why did a situation exist which led to these reactions under the natural laws, what happened before that, and you get back to the very hot universe I was talking about.

With these little heaps, you find that they were arranged by intelligent people to mark the track from one village to another. There is nothing more to be said; you have got finality for your fact. That is a trivial instance; but whenever you trace any event or observed fact to the action of intelligent purpose you have explained it; if you understand the purpose and sympathise with the object you are satisfied. So far as I am aware, there is no other principle in our experience about which this is true.

Faith in God is precisely the hypothesis that this one principle which is capable of offering a final explanation does in fact explain the universe. It starts intellectually with the proposition that here is the only chance of there being an explanation at all. Intellectually it is a hypothesis; but it is not by that road men have usually reached it. They have reached it by inner consciousness, and have transferred to the world about them what they found to be the explanation of their own conduct or that of their neighbours, or else through what they supposed to be personal communion with the Ultimate Being. Once they have posited a theory, it is there as a hypothesis to be tested, and the life of faith is the life of testing. Faith consists so far in the determination to live and to think as if this thing were true, and to find how far we can solve life's problems by the use of that hypothesis. We cannot hope to solve them all, for the range of the problems is the whole universe itself; but if we steadily make headway, that will be enough.

Let us turn to this world that we are seeking to explain, and look into its structure for a moment. The universe exists in a series of strata, one above the other, so to speak, or one imposed on the other. Of these there is an almost infinite variety, most delicately graded. But there are four main gradations which may be called matter, life, mind, and spirit. At the crown of them is personality; and the essence of personality is intelligent choice or purpose. If you think out what makes the difference between a person and a thing, or a person and a brute, you cannot escape that conclusion. The billiard ball only goes where you push it. That is the most humiliating fact in my experience; but it is true. If I could only suppose it had a will of its own, I should be much happier. Already, when you have reached the animal you have self-determination of a kind, but, as far as we can tell, it seems true that for the greater part of animal life such choice as exists is exercised in the choice of means to ends that are already fixed. A dog knows what he wants to eat, and thinks how to get it, but he does not choose between his ends. I am not dealing with the question of free-will and determinism. All I am concerned about is the difference which everyone recognises between being pushed into a river and jumping into a river.

When you jump into the river, the process of causation or determination has passed through your mind; you have become a deliberate and voluntary party to the act; but when you are pushed into the river, you are not a voluntary party to the act, as is proved by your emotional reaction. As you climb up the gradations of existence, as we know them, you reach intelligent choice in personality. What we already find to be the crown of the natural process, so far as it has gone, is just the thing we were saying might be the nature of the principle explaining the whole world.

There is a gulf between such personality as ours and the personality of God, or the personality that is in God. We are still aghast before the spectacle of the universe in which He operates. What some of our modern scientific thinkers are feeling is that the world is so vast that we cannot very much matter in it; and yet I know the stars are there, and if they are nothing more than Sir James Jeans has found out about them, they do not know I am here. I beat the stars. And when you come to those ranges of knowledge that the modern man has mastered and conquered, you see, however small his body may be, that by his mind he is greater than these merely measurable things, for he who measures is greater than that which he measures, even though his body is so much smaller.

When you come to the choice between the ends of life, which is the distinctive feature of the spiritual nature as against the merely intellectual, you discover a sense of obligation which is absolute, a sense of something which on every account I must do, or on no account must I do. In the reason and the conscience there is something which is demonstrably ultimate, and beyond which in principle it is not possible to go. Here we have something we may naturally expect to find akin to whatever is ultimate in the universe itself. God is not merely a word to represent the infinite power of the world, but the good that is there too. We shall have to consider later on how the mind recognises and appreciates goodness, whether in God or anywhere else; but I will anticipate now and dogmatize. Good or bad consists in the discovery by the mind of what is akin to or alien from itself in the thing it contemplates. Wherever you find the nature of mind answering your mind, there you have satisfaction. That is what we call good, and that at its height is love, so that if God is not only the supreme power but the supreme good, He must also be love; and we are ready for the revelation which came in Jesus Christ of God revealed as perfect love. And I want to leave you for this moment with the picture that St John gives of what our Lord did in a moment of special consciousness of His Divine mission and authority. Knowing that He came forth from God and went unto God, what did He do? He did not sit on a throne and invite His disciples to bow before Him in homage. He girded Himself and began to perform for them the act of service which was in that time and place regarded as the most menial that one man could do for another. That is what He thought it was like to be God. The Christian conception of God begins with an exaltation of the Divine Majesty, the greatest the mind can conceive, but when the greatness and the far-reaching power, might and authority of God exhibit themselves for man, it is by washing the disciples' feet.

Religious devotion has expressed itself as an aspiration to contemplate God:

> What rapture will it be
> Prostrate before Thy throne to lie
> And gaze and gaze on Thee.

Do we really think that would be rapture? If not, it is because we have forgotten what God is—the source of all Truth and all Beauty, in whom they are found in their completeness. That which is ultimate in us craves for the ultimate truth of reality, and can be satisfied with nothing else. This is to be wrought out in the good works of our lives. There are men who are brought to God through their effort to serve their neighbours. There are men who are inspired to serve their neighbours by their fellowship with God. But the two cannot be separated, and if either appears to be existing without the other there is something wrong in it.

That means that for us the fundamental business of life is always worship. At the root of all your being, your intellectual studies, the games you play, whatever it is, the impulse to do them well is and ought to be understood as being an impulse towards God, the source of all that is excellent. All life ought to be worship; and we know quite well there is no chance it will be worship unless we have times when we have worship and nothing else. No doubt when we are perfect, when fellowship with God is a constant realisation and joy, we shall not have to go backwards and forwards between times of worship and of the activities in which we show forth our loyalty to God; but we must do so now. Otherwise our interests in the world will cease for us to have any connection with God. It is our duty for a great part of the day to forget God, because if we are thinking about Him we shall not be thinking whole-heartedly about our duty in the world. Our duty to God requires that we should, for a good part of our time, be not consciously thinking about Him. That makes it absolutely necessary, if our life is to be a life of fellowship with Him, that we should have our times which are worship, pure and simple.

The test of these is whether, as a result of them, we have more love for our fellow-men. This is one of the differences between the emotional condition of real worship and the emotional condition generated by great art. They feel very much alike, but for many people at least the experience of great art creates a feeling of sensitiveness to the unsatisfying qualities of life and of our neighbours. When we have been absorbed in great music, I do not think we generally feel particularly charitable to the people we meet outside. They seem to be of a coarser fibre than that into which we have been entering. That could never be true of our worship if it has really been worship of God, not some indulgence of our own spiritual emotion, but the concentration of mind, heart and will on Him. You will be full of kindness for everybody as you go out from such worship. It is only as the world gets hold of you again that that begins to fail, and you have to come again and kindle the fire of your worship until it lasts undying.

People are always thinking that conduct is supremely important, and that because prayer helps it, therefore

prayer is good. That is true as far as it goes; still truer
is it to say that worship is of supreme importance and
conduct tests it. Conduct tests how much of yoursep
was in the worship you gave to God. You get most hellf
from religion when you have stopped thinking about
your needs, even for spiritual strength, and think about
God. Gaze and gaze on Him; let us then try to recall
to ourselves something of the majesty of God.

And Moses went up into the mount, and the cloud covered the
mount. And the glory of the Lord abode on mount Sinai, and the
cloud covered it six days: and the seventh day he called unto
Moses out of the midst of the cloud. And the appearance of the
glory of the Lord was like devouring fire on the top of the mount
in the eyes of the children of Israel.

And he said, Shew me, I pray thee, thy glory. And he said, I
will make all my goodness pass before thee, and will proclaim
the name of the Lord before thee: and I will be gracious to whom
I will be gracious, and will shew mercy on whom I will shew
mercy. And he said, Thou canst not see me and live.

And the Lord descended in the cloud, and stood with him there,
and proclaimed the name of the Lord. And the Lord passed before
him, and proclaimed, The Lord, the Lord, a God full of compas-
sion and gracious, slow to anger, and plenteous in mercy and
truth; keeping mercy for thousands, forgiving iniquity and trans-
gression and sin: and that will by no means clear the guilty;
visiting the iniquity of the fathers upon the children, and upon the
children's children, unto the third and fourth generation.

To whom then will ye liken me, that I shall be equal? saith the
Holy One. Lift up your eyes on high, and see who hath created
these, that bringeth out their host by number: he calleth them all
by name; by the greatness of his might, and for that he is strong
in power, not one is lacking. Why sayest thou, O Jacob, and
speakest, O Israel, My way is hid from the Lord, and my judgment

is passed away from my God? Hast thou not known? Hast thou not heard? The everlasting God, the Lord, the Creator of the ends of the earth, fainteth not, neither is weary; there is no searching of his understanding.

Thus saith the high and lofty One, that inhabiteth eternity, whose name is Holy: I dwell in the high and holy place, with him also that is of a contrite and humble spirit.

I am the Alpha and the Omega, saith the Lord God, which is and which was and which is to come, the Almighty.

Now unto the King eternal, incorruptible, invisible, the only God, be honour and glory for ever and ever. Amen.

2

THE PLACE OF CHRIST IN HISTORY

WE were thinking yesterday about God, the ultimate
reality, the union of absolute power and perfect goodness, whose purpose is the explanation of the world and
of all things in it, including our own lives. The discovery
of His purpose, therefore, and the conformity of our
own lives to it is the most important business in life.
We reflected that belief in such a God involves us also
in the belief that getting into the right relation with Him
is more important than anything else, and will carry
everything else that is important in its train. So worship
becomes the supreme business of life.

A great deal of worship has to be carried out in the
activities which we do not ordinarily think of as religious,
and in the doing of which we ought to be so occupied
with the task in hand that we are not consciously remembering God. In order that the performance of those
tasks may be duties to God at all, we need to be perpetually coming back to Him in times when He, and He
alone, occupies our thought and becomes the object to
which we offer the devotion of our souls.

But all this is very vague if that is all we have to say.
Those of you who are reading Aristotle's 'Ethics' will
be familiar with the observation that the intellect, by
itself, sets nothing in motion. Merely to think things are
one's duty or are good, without at the same time feeling

them as good and obligatory, is not enough to control conduct. We have somehow to cross over from this, however accurate, yet shadowy and vague, conception of the Divine, into something which has compelling power. That is the reason why men make idols.

Originally when men made images, that marked a great religious advance. Then images began to be a hindrance, because the image was inadequate. It never really represented the truth about God and, above all, it could not represent Him as the living God. The image is static, unchangeable, the same in all relationships. It will not show the sign of life—reaction with an infinite delicacy to all the variations of circumstance and context.

Phidias tried to produce an image more beautiful than any human form could ever be; Plato said that was the artist's true aim. But when all is said and done, the exquisite statue remains for ever the same, and any living human form is superior to it. That is one reason, no doubt, why Israel was forbidden to make images, though here there was the further consideration that the images likely to be made would be of animals; as the Psalmist satirically observed, 'They turned their glory into the similitude of a calf that eateth hay.' The prophetic denunciations have no direct application to the artistic masterpieces of the Greeks.

It remains true that any image is inadequate; but what people often fail to observe is that when, instead of making the image out of material things, you make it out of thoughts, if you make it yourself, it will be equally inadequate, and it is just as much idolatry to worship God according to a false mental image as by means of

a false metal image. The mental image misrepresents
God, and has the same disastrous effects on character.
If your conception of God is radically false, then the
more devout you are the worse it will be for you. You
are opening your soul to be moulded by something base.
You had much better be an atheist.

There is a possibility that a revelation of God should
come through human nature, just because that human
nature is in the image of God, in the sense that in reason
and in conscience man has something which is ultimate
in nature and principle. Beyond what is universal and
absolute you cannot go, and therefore in principle a
revelation through human nature is possible, and the
Gospel consists of the proclamation that it has happened.
Always remember that Jesus Christ is offered to men
first and foremost, not as a problem but as a solution.
The problem is how are we to conceive God more fully
and perfectly so as to obtain that grip, as it were, on
the Divine nature which shall enable it to obtain a grip
on us. We do not start with the life recorded in the
Gospels and ask, 'What are you going to say about it?
Is it not really so marvellous that you are bound to call
Him Divine?' But if we follow the line in which the
revelation was actually given, we shall say instead, 'The
world is governed somehow; there is a rational principle
at work in it; and the character of that principle is seen
in Jesus Christ.'

Whenever we lay our plans, thinking out the consequences of the experience we have and of the actions
we contemplate, we are presupposing that this world is
governed by a rational principle to which our own

actions are akin, so that we can trace out those workings. The name for that rational principle in that day was the *logos*. It had two meanings, and it meant them both. It meant this rational principle that governs the world, and also the utterance of God by which He created the world.

Do not perplex yourself with everything that is written in introductions to St John's Gospel, discussing whether St John's *logos* is the Stoic *logos* or the Hebrew *Memra*; he certainly meant both, and he certainly thought they were the same. The rational principle that governs the world is the utterance of the mind of God—the mind of God expressing itself in outward form uttering itself; and our understanding of it is very limited. But it is really impossible to doubt that it is there. St John says we know the character of this *logos*. The principle that governs the universe 'became flesh and dwelt among us and we beheld His glory,' and the impression was as of something that shone through Him from beyond—'glory as of an Only Begotten Son from a Father'; of One who perfectly represented something and who is perfectly united with it. So the Fourth Gospel, which by common consent at least represents the tradition handed down by the beloved disciple, helps us to understand the person of our Lord.

The interest of all the questions asked about Him by Christians is fundamentally due to their bearing on another question—namely, the question about God. The doctrine of the Incarnation is not first and foremost of importance because of what it says about Somebody who lived in Palestine; it is of fundamental importance be-

cause of what it tells us about the eternal and unchanging
God, who is and always will be Himself; and if He, in
His self-expression, has given perfect expression of His
character in terms of human life, then as we look at that
life we see the Eternal God. And if the world we know,
or any finite world, is to be God's world, it must be
because somehow He gives Himself to it. It cannot perfectly correspond to His infinite purpose except by virtue
of the Infinite and the Eternal dwelling in it and giving
it His own power.

Here, as so often, there are two thoughts both necessary which you have to hold in a true balance. There
is no man in the world in whom this *logos*, this Word of
God, this rational principle of all things, does not speak.
The veriest atheist of them all thinks by the power of
that which is perfectly revealed in Jesus Christ. It is the
light that lighteth every man. You never get away from
it, and there is nobody who is without it. That light
which lighteth every man, and which shone by fits and
starts elsewhere, that Word which was spoken in divers
portions and divers manners in the prophets, shone out
supremely and found perfect utterance in the Son. He
is the Son of God in that sense (among others) in which
we say of a man that he is the son of his father, meaning
that in him the father's character is reproduced. So
supremely is our Lord the Son because in Him we truly
see the Father.

And so the light is indeed in every man, and there is
no man who is entirely separate from Christ, from the
Word which is Christ. But it makes all the difference in
the world if the individual finds it out or not; whether

he ever turns his gaze towards the perfection of the thing which is best in himself. The mind grows always by intercourse with a mind more mature than itself. That is the secret of all teaching. If what is Divine in us, that image of God stamped on us in reason and conscience, is to become all it can be, it must be through intercourse with those in whom that element is more maturely developed. It must be by fellowship with Him in whom alone it appears in perfection.

But can the perfect be already come? Our forefathers used to debate with anxiety how it came about that the supreme revelation was so long postponed; Gibbon made a good deal of fun about that. Nowadays people are liable to ask, not how it came so late, but how it could possibly come so early. Is it not always true that the best is yet to be? Well, Yes, in a certain sense, and quite equally No in certain other senses.

In science it is true that the later supersedes the earlier; it is not true in art. Nobody supposes that, when perfect expression of some human emotion has once been given, it will ever be thrown upon the scrap-heap, because someone a hundred years later may do it again. He may do it again, but he will never do it better. What is the most indispensable condition for moral progress, which is the thing here in point? The most indispensable condition is that you should know which way to go. If you are always changing your direction, you never get any farther, and one reason why the last fifty years have been so barren of effective political progress is that people have been constantly changing their direction. There may be good reasons for changing our direction, but it is an advantage and not a loss that you should really know the way, and that you should go that way.

'I am the way,' said Christ, and what is offered is not the goal of history, but the direction in which history should move, and the power which should carry it forward.

What is claimed is that there has been given to men perfect representation of the true principles of life at its root. It is not a claim to have revealed all the secrets, either of science or statesmanship. Christ was not a statesman; He refused to deal with those problems. Christ was not in the ordinary sense an artist, though He had the most profound appreciation of beauty, and His appreciation has become the standard for very much of the world's taste until now, and will remain so. But these are departments of life on which He did not specifically enter.

It is the fundamental relationship of man to God with which He is concerned. It is that principle which the Gospel claims as being revealed in Him, and which we have progressively to apply in one department of life after another.

There is another kind of problem that we must raise. Are we justified in supposing that God really does certain particular things in a special manner, or that you can call them His activity in a sense in which other events are not? That is perhaps less difficult than it was a generation ago, because we have become entirely used to the notion that there certainly have been breaches in the continuity of the world's development, and today, for the moment, breaches of continuity are regarded as occurring at the very foundation of all physical existence. The quantum theory, for instance, holds that there are a number of changes happening in the atomic sphere of which there is at present no scientific explanation at all. It is surely quite clear that if anyone studied the world before there was life on it he could never have predicted life; if he had studied vegetation he would never have predicted animal life; if he had studied the animal world he would never have predicted human civilisation and the arts; and if he had studied the selfishness of mankind he could never have predicted a life of perfect and selfless love. At each such stage we reasonably trace the special activity of the Will whose purpose is the explanation of all things.

Now let us stop and ask for a moment whether we can see the character of that life and consider its outline. Our Lord came to people trained on the Old Testament. He was Himself brought up in the piety of the Israelite home, with the Old Testament as His sacred literature; and the Old Testament had fostered the hope of the coming Messiah, who would inaugurate the Kingdom of God. There were various conceptions of how it would be done, and even what the thing would be when it was done; but the terms, 'Messiah' and 'Kingdom of God,' go together. At His Baptism, if not before, He became convinced in the experience of the voice from heaven speaking to Him in the Messianic text, 'This is my beloved Son . . .' that He was as Messiah to begin the work of inaugurating the Kingdom.

Being such, He is endowed with the power of God for the purpose of God, and at once He faces three temptations. What are they? Incidentally, they arise out of the Old Testament. The first comes from the expectation of the Messianic banquet, the second from the conception of the King ruling from Jerusalem, and the third from the conception of the Son of Man giving His sign from heaven, overcoming resistance by irresistible evidence of His authority. There is the hope of a 'good time coming' when all desires will be satisfied; there is the thought of authority compelling obedience to its righteous commands by force; and there is the notion of such manifestation of divine authority as would make resistance so foolish as to be impossible. Each of these presents itself as a way of establishing the Kingdom. What is their common quality? They are three ways, and the only three ways, in which the conduct of men can be controlled without winning their loyalty. Bribery, appealing to their natural desires; force, which secures obedience by making it not worth while to disobey; and overwhelming evidence which affords such demonstration of the claim presented that it becomes foolishness to resist it. Those are the three things which in the wilderness He considered and turned down; and what form of the Messianic expectation has He left? He left nothing; none of the earlier expectations survive at all; for I am persuaded that He discarded the apocalyptic expectation as completely as the other two. He has left nothing. He goes forth among men living the life of perfect love. He is possessed of power which He uses always for love's sake, and never in any other way. The crowds become excited because of His works of wonder, and He does not want them so. Then He does two things. He speaks the Parable of the Sower, describing His ministry up to date. He has been scattering the proclamation of the coming Kingdom, and here and there it has taken root for a while and withered; here and there it has never taken root at all; only here and there it has found the soil in which it could grow. Such a conception of the Kingdom was quite incredible to Jews trained on the Old Testament. And so He applies to them the words of Isaiah about seeing and not perceiving, while to the disciples He explains the mystery—the secret—of the Kingdom of God.

At this same time He chooses twelve men to be His companions, that they may learn to understand Him; and He takes them on two walking tours—of all human enterprises the most productive of intimacy. There is little told us about those journeys because they were out of the region of controversy, which is, no doubt, why He went there. Therefore there is little to recall. Then He thinks they have come to understand, and says to Peter, 'Who say men that I am?' They mention all the popular guesses. 'Who say ye that I am?' And then Peter answers, 'Thou art the Messiah,' the promised founder of the Kingdom of God.

The moment He has been recognised, our Lord does two things. He says repeatedly what He has never said before: 'The Son of Man must suffer.' There is the great thing He will do; the Son of Man, the title of the Messiah in His glory, will suffer. God is love; glory is the shining forth of His nature; then the Sacrifice of Christ is the highest glory of God.

As He began to give that teaching, so He began that

journey to Jerusalem, at the end of which He would challenge the High Priests and authorities and precipitate the Passion. The Son of Man must suffer because sacrifice is the real expression of love; and God, whose Kingdom He came to found, is first and foremost a God of Love, and the response He seeks is the response that loving hearts give to love which has shown itself in sacrifice for them.

Through this ministry He does things which are plainly Divine. As we read, the story is not of One going about with the consciousness of the Divinity on Him, though He has the consciousness of a relationship with God, His Father, such as He does not find in other men, and is able to claim that He alone can declare the Father. Yet He does things which are Divine, but it is with an absence of any trace of arrogance in Himself, or a feeling of arrogance in Him on the part of others; more particularly He acts as Divine when He deliberately rewrites the Divine Law. Try to conceive what was involved for a devout Jew in taking the Law of Moses and rewriting it!

All through, what we seem to witness is a life which is human indeed, human to the very uttermost. But that is never the last word about it. Always working through it, sometimes apparently breaking the human mould, there comes the Divine power from beyond, so that as men thought of what He was like, they said that, as they were with Him, they beheld His glory, the glory as of an only begotten Son from a Father, unconscious of anything that separated Him from God, and thereby different from every saint in every part of the world. In Him there is the sense of the perfectly continuous intimacy with the Father, an intimacy in which He can act in respect of every relationship of life as it arises with an absolute confidence and sureness of touch.

He does not have to rely on the authority of the past or on other teachers. It is in Himself. He acts with the manifest authority of God; He is the creative Word of God. In Him we are to see what is the purpose of God in making the world and in making us. As this is shown in our own nature, He becomes the Head of our race in whom we can each find himself.

Remember that Christianity is not, first and foremost, a religion; it is first and foremost a revelation. It comes before us chiefly not with a declaration of feelings we are to cultivate, or thoughts we are to develop; it comes before us, first and foremost, with the announcement of what God is, as He is proved in what He has done.

He comes before us commanding still, but not only commanding—pleading. He asks not only for our obedience, but for our sympathy; what He wants above all things else is our affection—that our desire may be to do what will please Him. When we feel like that towards anyone on earth we call it loving him. We are to reach the point when we desire to do what pleases God for no reason beyond. We can do it in His fellowship—not without.

The test of our belief is always in our practice. There are a great many of us who profess a belief in God and His supreme revelation of Himself in Jesus Christ. At any rate, we should be quite firm in our refusal to deny it. Then we go on as if nothing had happened. Yet if this great thing is true it will be the most ordinary common sense that we should perpetually come back to Him to check all our thoughts, all our desires, and all our plans.

What we cannot expect to happen is that our characters are going to change through our holding an opinion which we keep somewhere in a pigeon-hole of the mind merely to be brought out on demand. You say the Creed; the words, 'I believe in God,' do not mean, 'I incline to the opinion that in all probability there exists a Being who may not inappropriately be called God.' You mean, 'I put my trust in that union of power and goodness.' You mean, 'I undertake to live as if these things were so.' If you do not mean that, you ought not to say the Creed.

Our characters are shaped by our companions and by the objects to which we give most of our thoughts and with which we fill our imaginations. We cannot always be thinking even about Christ, but we can refuse to dwell on any thoughts which are out of tune with Him. We can, above all, quite deliberately turn our minds towards Him at any time when those thoughts come in.

You will find it is not possible for a vivid memory of Jesus Christ and an unclean thought or a mean and treacherous desire to be in your mind at the same time. It cannot happen. What we have to drill ourselves in—it means drill—is quite constantly to bring our minds, thoughts, desires, hopes, plans, and ambitions back to the touch-stone: will they stand without discord in His presence? We must begin with prayer, because if you are selfish in your prayers there is not much hope that you will be really unselfish anywhere else. I think some people are more selfish in their prayers than in their action, because they let themselves drift into a habit of prayer which does not correspond with their general outlook. Still, if you are selfish in your prayers there is not much hope.

Ambition! What are you going to do with your lives? To choose your career for selfish reasons is a worse sin than, let us say, committing adultery, for it is the withdrawal of the greater part of your time and energy from the service of God. Of course you are not going to be turned out of a club for doing it, but you will turn yourself out of the fellowship of Christ by doing it. It is very often true that our inclinations are a sure guide to our vocation, for we like doing what we can do well; but the reason why we ought to do it is that it will be of more use, not that we shall like it better. Our motive in taking up an occupation should be to serve.

What does your mind run on when there is no reason why it should run on anything? What does it turn to spontaneously when you wake in the morning? It must be in tune with Christ.

Hope! Apart from your ambition for yourself, what are you looking forward to? Christian Hope is the consecration of desire, and desire is the hardest thing of all to consecrate. When you positively hope for the Kingdom of God, then your desire becomes consecrated. That will only happen as you begin to think how lovely the life according to Christ is. You will only find that out by getting to know Him very well. It is as you dwell

with Christ and let your mind become subdued to Him
that you begin to see how lovely a thing it is. But, again,
you must not be selfish about it. Remember that Christianity is not just another religion of individual salvation,
differing only in having a different plan of salvation to
offer. It is the one and only religion of world-redemption.
We are members of the family of God; when we come
to Him in Christ, it must always be in the company of
our brothers and sisters. We must not come alone; we
have no right to be there alone.

As we check our thoughts and desires in these ways,
we shall become over and over again desperately ashamed
and humiliated; but we shall always find every time we
really honestly face the comparison between His life and
ours that we not only see the difference, but quite genuinely perceive the effect of His transforming touch.
He can change people into His own likeness. It is not
only that He stimulates us, as other great men stimulate
us, but we find a power coming from Him into our lives
that enables us to respond. That is the experience that
proves Him to be the universal Spirit. It does not happen
with others.

When we dwell upon the figure of Christ, we are at
once in contact with something which embraces us here
and now, the eternal Spirit of God pervading and
sustaining all things. It is His.

Have this mind in you which also is in Christ Jesus: who, being
in the form of God, counted it not a prize to be on equality with
God, but emptied himself, taking the form of a servant, being
made in the likeness of men; and being found in fashion as a man,
he humbled himself, becoming obedient even unto death, yea, the

death of the cross. Wherefore also God highly exalted him, and gave unto him the name which is above every name; that in the name of Jesus every knee should bow, of things in heaven and things on earth and things under the earth, and that every tongue should confess that Jesus Christ is Lord, to the glory of God the Father.

But one hath somewhere testified saying,
What is man, that thou art mindful of him?
Or the son of man, that thou visitest him?
Thou madest him a little lower than the angels;
Thou crownedst him with glory and honour,
And didst set him over the works of thy hands:
Thou didst put all things in subjection under his feet.

For in that he subjected all things unto him, he left nothing that is not subject to him. But now we see not yet all things subjected to him. But we behold him who hath been made a little lower than the angels, even Jesus, because of the suffering of death, crowned with glory and honour, that by the grace of God he should taste death for every man. For it became him, for whom are all things, and through whom are all things, in bringing many sons unto glory, to make the author of their salvation perfect through sufferings.

Having then a great high priest, who hath passed through the heavens, Jesus the Son of God, let us hold fast our confession. For we have not a high priest that cannot be touched with the feeling of our infirmities; but one that hath been in all points tempted like as we are, yet without sin. Let us therefore draw near with boldness unto the throne of grace, that we may receive mercy, and may find grace to help us in time of need.

Having therefore, brethren, boldness to enter into the holy place by the blood of Jesus, by the way which he dedicated for us, a new and living way, through the veil, that is to say, his flesh; and having a great priest over the house of God; let us draw near with a true heart in fullness of faith.

Beloved, now are we children of God, and it is not yet made

manifest what we shall be. We know that, if he shall be manifested we shall be like him, for we shall see him even as he is.

Now unto him that is able to do exceeding abundantly above all that we ask or think, according to the power that worketh in us, unto him be glory in the Church by Christ Jesus throughout all ages, world without end. Amen.

3

IS THERE A MORAL STANDARD?

A GREAT general upheaval, like that of the war, inevitably leads men to re-examine with a fresh eagerness of criticism everything which may be regarded as in some degree responsible for leading up to that event. One often meets people who feel that everything which belonged to the pre-war world is discredited because the accepted beliefs and practices of that world were powerless to prevent the immense catastrophe of the war, and the almost equally immense catastrophe of the form which the peace has taken.

Nothing comes under this new criticism more fully than everything which might be regarded as a moral convention. This does not in the least mean that people, in their practice, are more remote than their predecessors from the conventions which we accepted before the war; probably they are in some respects more remote, and in some respects less so. What is quite certain is that they have an active doubt about the standards by which these things used to be confidently settled. There is on all sides a collapse of authority, but especially of spiritual and moral authority.

People recognise that civic authority, for example, has at any rate a utilitarian value. It is necessary for people living at close quarters to have some regulations to govern their intercourse with one another, and if there are regulations they must in some degree be enforced. There is not much doubt about the value of some form of government. The answers you would get from thinking people today to the question, 'Why should we obey the law?' would, I think, be very much more utilitarian than they would have been twenty years ago. Where the utilitarian value is not obvious, the claim tends to be set almost entirely on one side, and we are left with the question whether there is or is not any standard of moral judgment which can make good its claim on us.

Now, in this collapse of any generally accepted moral standard, we do not find that men are trying to live without some forms of moral principle. If we take that sort of literature which is in many ways most remote from Victorian standards, we do not find it is devoid of any ethical system. I am not very widely read in that kind of literature, but the books I have read leave a very clear impression on my mind. The writers take it for granted that no sensible person has any object in life except enjoyment, and that you may pursue your enjoyment in any way that is agreeable to yourself, except when it interferes with the similar enjoyment of people in your own set. It would hardly be said perhaps that you are obliged to forgo your enjoyment when it would interfere with that of other people in your own set, but there is open admiration for those who are ready to give up their enjoyment, even indeed to expose themselves to great endurance and abandon life itself, rather than interfere with the enjoyment of other people in the same set.

The kind of folk mostly depicted in these books are

folk whose whole manner of life would be quite impossible if there were not, behind the scenes so to speak,
what are sometimes spoken of as 'the toiling masses.'
The life of these hedonistic butterflies is only made
possible by somebody producing the wealth that they
squander. It is never suggested that they do or should
consider their obligation to the folk by whose labour
they exist. Nevertheless, there remain the elements of a
moral system. Even if it is not obligatory, at least it is
admirable, to forgo your own enjoyment for the sake
of increasing, or avoiding the diminution of, the enjoyment of other people in your own set.

I believe a great deal of the confusion that exists arises
from beginning inquiry at what seems to be the wrong
end. It is very natural, because the moral conventions
of society are apt to present themselves to us as restric-
tions on our opportunities to enjoy ourselves. There
are things that we want to do, and we are told that we
must not do. We ask, 'Why not?' and we are told that
it would be wrong. There was a time when to be told
something was wrong, if it was said in a sufficiently
appropriate tone of voice, produced a kind of respon-
siveness in those to whom it was said. But when once
the spirit of criticism has become very prevalent, that
stops; and when people are told something is wrong,
they say, 'But what is wrong about it?' or 'Why is it
wrong? what is the standard which condemns it?'

There are no general negative rules about morals
which are fit for universal acceptance, unless they are
so formed as to include reference to motive or to particular conditions. For example, we may be content to say

that murder is always wrong, but that is because murder is a kind of killing which is wrong. But not all killing is wrong. By common consent there are cases of justifiable homicide. Murder is always wrong; only is it murder? Some cases are clear enough, and I do not think that the repudiation of conventional ethics has gone the length of justifying real murder for the sake of increasing one's own enjoyment.

But we are not getting any nearer our standard. All these things which are condemned are condemned by reference to something, and that something must be positive. The primitive ethical codes of all nations are mainly negative. That is because people—though they might not yet be able to formulate the principle of the right way of life—yet have, by long experience, found out that this, that, and the other actions are not compatible with it. That is how the negative rules, such as we have in most of the Decalogue, get built up. They are the deposit of the accumulated experience of the tribe or race regarding its experience that such and such courses of conduct do, in fact, result in disaster if they are permitted to become frequent in society.

Plainly, this implies the assumption of some kind of life for which the tribe or race is groping and has not found. The perplexity is increased because, as people go about the world, they find that these tribal customs are different in different places. By what standard are you going to say that one is right and the other wrong? No doubt, it is a very serious matter to offend against any convention on which the social structure is based, because you are going to cause some dislocation, and if many people do it, there will be great dislocation. But is that all that can be said?

The variety of ethical codes in different parts of the world presupposes agreement in one thing, namely, that there is a difference between right and wrong. People may call some things right in some parts of the world which are called wrong in another part of the world; but the difference between right and wrong remains. Is this anything else but conformity with that which has been built up by each group or tribe in its experience of life?

If you are going to take up one restriction after another and ask, 'Is there any inherent sanctity in this?' you will never find one that has any. It is not there that moral authority resides; it resides rather in the comparative estimate of the various good things which you may try to secure. Thus, for example, those good things which are enjoyed by means of our distinctively human capacity belong to a higher order than those which we enjoy by the capacities we share with the animals. The difference between the human race and the animals consists in the addition to all the animal nature of various other qualities. It is quite plain that that is where the difference is. Man's capacity to think and to imagine, to plan and purpose—all of these things are new, and therefore the kinds of good sought by these are kinds of good, towards the appreciation of which nature has been working through the upward striving of its evolutionary course.

Incidentally, if the spiritual nature of man belongs to the eternal world, then the goods appreciated by means of it also have the added advantage that they are capable of an eternal enjoyment, which is certainly not true of animal pleasures. As these personal qualities are the highest thing about us, and are capable of regulating the others, as the others cannot regulate them, so it is at least natural to suggest that the highest of all goods in life consists of personal relations; and there are very few people in fact who will dispute that. It is not possible to say that other things, like knowledge or beauty, are good only in so far as they promote personal relationship, but because there is not in them the intercourse of mind with mind in its most intense form, they are not quite on the same level of value.

If anyone disputes that and says, 'As far as I can tell, animal enjoyments are exactly as good as any other enjoyment, only some people prefer one and some prefer the other,' we have for our answer at least this reference to the course of evolution itself; and we have the reference to the possession of these things through eternity if we believe in that. But, in the last resort, I admit that is all. The judgment of value is, in the last resort, what is sometimes called intuitive. You see it or you do not, and there is no getting past that. Only we complicate the issue dreadfully if we try to apply this immediate judgment, not only to the general goal and fundamental principle of life, but also to all particular acts.

Particular acts derive their value from their capacity to promote or to hinder the best relations between people, the relationship which must express their personality. All particular commands or prohibitions derive their value from their tendency to promote or to hinder the relationship of love on the widest possible scale;

and all value judgments, in the last resort, are forms
of this. There have been many schools, as you know,
of moral philosophy, and I want to suggest to you that
the thing which really helps is to get quite clear which
things are means to ends, and which are ends in themselves. If we are to have any clear view at all, we must
settle what is the thing we are aiming at, which we
want for itself alone.

Even knowledge and beauty are heightened when they
are shared, and, in the common enjoyment, provide a
link uniting the two personalities together in a relationship which most people find more precious than the
experience which united them. But whether or not it is
possible in this way to relate knowledge and beauty to
love, as the true relationship between persons, it is
broadly true, I suggest, that we ought to imply in every
moral judgment that the aim of life is to promote this
ideal relationship between people. We do not always
think of it like that. None the less the principle is there.
In other words the fundamental moral law is, 'Thou
shalt love thy neighbour as thyself.'

Then we turn from that for a moment to some of the
conventions that have come down to us, and ask, What
is our attitude to them? And, if we are Christians, we
shall draw a very sharp distinction between those which
have grown up under Christian influence and those that
have not. About those that have grown up under
Christian influence we shall say, 'They have a great *prima
facie* authority. We must not set them aside unless we
can find ground for setting them aside in the very principle they aim at expressing.'

Take, for illustration, the laws which govern property. You may, for example, argue like this: What justifies property and the safeguarding of its rights is that it makes personality fuller, it enables a man to live a fuller life, expressing himself in a greater variety of ways, and therefore it is good for persons to have property. But if so, then it must be good for all persons to have property; and therefore a law of property which results in a few persons having property and the others hardly any cannot be a good law of property.

The place where the modern mind has changed most in relation to the Victorian mind is in relation to sex. There was a quite clear suggestion that sex is in its own nature really evil, and only becomes justified when used for the propagation of the species; but it is not permissible for any Christian to say that anything that God made is inherently evil. Incidentally, when St John wanted to make his great proclamation he did not say, 'The Word became man'; he deliberately took the word which represents the lowest elements in human nature and said, 'The Word became flesh.'

It seems to me we have, in a certain sense, to make a new start about this, and begin with the recognition of the complete wholesomeness of the natural fact of sex. Then we must go on and ask why our predecessors held the other view. It is never right to rest content with disproving another man's view. You must always go on to ask why he held it. You must say, 'He is sure to have got hold of something important; he put it wrong, but what was it he had got hold of?' The sum of what he had got hold of here was that sex, being a strong natural appetite in animals, and being enormously strengthened in man by the use of imagination, is very liable in human nature to grow in a degree entirely disproportionate. So there is a peculiar difficulty in maintaining, in this respect, that true economy of nature in which to every impulse there is given its own proper, but no more than its own proper, exercise. If our ancestors were wrong in their suggestions that there was about sex something wrong, they were quite right in thinking there was about it something which gave the greatest ground for the most anxious caution.

It is to be recognised that sex is holy as well as wholesome. It is the means by which we may bring into the world—not only as with the animal creation others of our biological species—it is the means by which we may co-operate with God in bringing into the world children of His own destined for eternal life. Anyone, who has once understood that, will be quite as careful as any Puritan to avoid making jokes about sex; not because it is nasty, but because it is sacred. He would no more joke about sex than he would joke about the Holy Communion—and for exactly the same reason. To joke about it is to treat with lightness something that deserves reverence.

These are the lines on which we have to readjust a good deal of our thinking about these things. And we find, as we study the teaching of the New Testament in this regard, that it all rests on one quite clear principle. The union of the sexes physically can only be right when it is the expression of a spiritual union of such a quality that it is inevitably lifelong. If you put together the things said by our Lord and by St Paul on this subject, you will find the principle which holds them together is that this union should be, and is meant to be, an expression of a spiritual union so complete that it must be lifelong.

From that all the rest will be bound to follow; let us always begin with our ultimate principle. Find out what it is and argue from it. Do not begin with particular enactments, or say, 'What is the sanctity of this?'

Let us also recognise that what we obtain through Christian belief is just the fundamentals, and nothing else; and that there may be, in many respects, a considerable variety. People sometimes want the Gospel to give them a quite clear standard by which to judge the question, for example, whether a man should devote himself to his art, even though by means of it he can hardly earn a penny, or whether he should throw it up and take up some other occupation, in which he is not fulfilling what he thinks to be the Divine call of his own nature, so as better to support his family. There is no general answer to questions like that, and there cannot be.

But what is also true is this: if we are thinking of these things, not merely on the grounds of morals, but on the grounds of religion, we shall know that God is our Father and the Father of all men, and that His Will is our welfare and theirs. Over and over again it will happen that if a man, having thought out such a problem to the best of his ability, will then lay the whole matter in the hands of God, and genuinely desire that God's Will shall be done in his life and not his own, he will become perfectly clear what that will is. Over and over again that happens.

Of course, talking about these things in general terms is rather futile. Do not think me egoistic if I give you one experience of my own. I had once to make a choice which I found very difficult. I was much interested in the work I was doing, believing it to be of some value. I was asked to take up another post which certainly was more conspicuous in the eyes of the world. I tried to avoid it. I asked all the friends of whom I could think, and they all said that I had better stay where I was. I had to make a decision in time to write a letter by a certain post, and having weighed up the question as carefully as I could—and we must always do that—and having come to no conclusion at all, I began at eight o'clock in the evening to say my prayers, and for three hours, without a pause, I tried to concentrate all my desires on knowing clearly what was God's Will for me. I do not know how those three hours went; they did not seem very long; but when eleven o'clock struck I knew perfectly well what I had got to do, and that was to accept; and I have never had a shadow of doubt since that it was right. One might go on. Other people, of course, have experiences far more striking and intimate. But there the thing is; there is no one general rule that settles these things for everyone. Each man has to find his own vocation. Every man is able to find that out if, quite sincerely, he will seek to do, not his own will, but God's.

There is one group of problems now becoming supremely important, about which we have not yet found our principles. Let us recognise them in order that we may not be confused. They are the problems of the relationship between the great groups of men. You often hear it said, what is morally wrong cannot be politically right. What people mean when they say it is usually that no nation, for example, ought to treat another nation in a different way from that in which one individual ought to treat another. I am sure that is not true; but we have no satisfactory theory to set against it. We have not yet found the principles; the League of Nations is doing that. We have not yet worked out what ought to be the relation of a trade union to an employers' federation, or vice versa. It is not just the same as that of one individual to another individual. All this still wants working out. Perhaps some of you are going to help in working it out. There are few things to which a man could better dedicate his mind than these.

Such gaps in our ethical theory do not throw discredit, however, on the fundamental and ultimate principle to which we now come back. We are speaking here as Christians; that is to say, as people who believe that God, the Supreme Reality in whom perfect good is to be found as well as absolute power, has revealed Himself. There is given a revelation of Him; in what form? Not in a code, not in a set of rules, but in a Person. And what Christ reveals in His own Person is the proper relation between man and God, and the proper relation between one man and another consequent upon their proper relationship to God.

He gives no solution of problems of statesmanship, or of economics, or of æsthetics, though His fundamental principle has its bearing on all of these. But He is not concerned with them. He is concerned only with what is universal and fundamental. I do not think you can say that a man who is devoting all his faculties to science will be a better scientist if he becomes a Christian, though he will be a more complete man. I should find it hard to say that an artist would necessarily become a better artist by becoming a Christian, though I should expect it to result in some greater refinement in his art. But whatever we are going to do, we must do it in relationship to God and in relationship to our fellow-men. And here the revelation given in Christ is directly relevant. The standard of morals is the mind of Christ; that is our great principle if we are Christian. It will not help you at once to solve each particular problem; it will give you a touch-stone. As you seek to live in the constant companionship of Christ, you will find yourself knowing ever more fully what your duty is in accordance with His mind. Your moral authority is not a principle, but a Person. It is the mind of Christ.

Our moral standard is the mind of Christ, and there have been very few who will venture to criticise it. In fact, as you study it, as you put it before your conscience, your conscience responds. But if that is the standard, and we are sincere about it, of course the immediate result is a sense of desperate humiliation. Mostly, when people argue about moral standards, what they are wanting to know is the authority for the rules they are expected to keep. What the Gospel tells you is the standard to which you must increasingly approximate. Some people say they do not need religion: do not need it for what? You do not need religion to make you as good as the world requires you to be; the help of the world itself is enough for that. You begin to feel the need of it when you have a vision of Christ as the standard for yourself and of the world as it might be, the world as it is in the mind of Christ, the kind of world that Christ died to make. Then you know that the kind of person you are may be perfectly satisfactory to your fellow-men, and to yourself until that vision came. But it is not going to help to bring that vision true. On the contrary, it is because people are like us that the world is what it is. That is the source of all the trouble.

The worst things that happen do not happen because a few people are monstrously wicked, but because most people are like us. When we grasp that, we begin to realise that our need is not merely for moving quietly on in the way we are going; our need is for radical change, to find a power that is going to turn us into somebody else. That is what the Gospel offers to do; and it delivers us, once and for all, from the desperate folly of making experiments in the moral life. Always remember, when you experiment with your soul, that you can never judge the result. No crime looks so bad to the man who has committed it as to the man who has kept clear of it. As soon as we have done something that is nasty, we have blunted our own capacity to be disgusted, we have tarnished the mirror in which we are to look at our own reflection. If the standard by which we are going to try to judge and guide our lives is the mind of Christ, then we are going to try to live in constant fellowship with Him and in company with others who are seeking that fellowship with Him.

We shall make this the main business of our lives. It will become a bond of unity binding us to others who have the same aim, and communion with Christ in the fellowship of His servants will have become the means by which we try to apply the moral standard to ourselves.

This commandment which I command thee this day, it is not too hard for thee, neither is it far off. It is not in heaven, that thou shouldest say, Who shall go up for us to heaven, and bring it unto us, and make us to hear it, that we may do it? Neither is it beyond the sea, that thou shouldest say, Who shall go over the sea for us, and bring it unto us, and make us to hear it, that we may do it? But the word is very nigh unto thee, in thy mouth, and in thy heart, that thou mayest do it.

I call heaven and earth to witness against you this day, that I have set before thee life and death, the blessing and the curse: therefore choose life.

The lamp of the body is the eye: if therefore thine eye be single, thy whole body shall be full of light. But if thine eye be evil, thy whole body shall be full of darkness. If therefore the light that is in thee be darkness, how great is the darkness!

For God sent not the Son into the world to judge the world; but that the world should be saved through him. He that believeth on him is not judged: he that believeth not hath been judged already, because he hath not believed on the name of the only begotten Son of God. And this is the judgment, that the light is come into the world, and men loved the darkness rather than the light; for their works were evil.

And Jesus said, For judgment came I into this world, that they which see not may see; and that they which see may become blind. Those of the Pharisees which were with him heard these things, and said unto him, Are we also blind? Jesus said unto them, If ye were blind, ye would have no sin: but now ye say, We see: your sin remaineth.

Beloved, now we are children of God, and it is not yet made manifest what we shall be. We know that, if he shall be manifested, we shall be like him; for we shall see him even as he is. And every one that hath this hope set on him purifieth himself, even as he is pure.

Now unto him that is able to guard you from stumbling, and to set you before the presence of his glory without blemish in exceeding joy, to the only God our Saviour, through Jesus Christ our Lord, be glory, majesty, dominion and power, before all time, and now, and for evermore. Amen.

4

SIN AND REPENTANCE

WE have tried to bring before our minds the thought of God as the union of absolute power with perfect goodness—Creator, Ruler, Sustainer of the world, who has created all things, for whose pleasure they are and were created. We have thought of the universe as existing in accordance with His thought, His thought expressed therein—that is to say, His Word, apart from which there has not been anything made that was made. We have meditated upon the proclamation of the Gospel, that this Word is made known to us in Jesus Christ; we have considered the mind of Christ as supplying us, in the last resort, with our moral standard; not in the last resort only as we have occasion to refer to it, but in the sense that it is the final reference on all occasions. And then that whole fabric, and that whole hope, seems to be upset because across the whole universe lies the blight of evil.

Perhaps that is too much to say, because I do not know that any of the curious behaviour detected by modern science in nebulæ could be called evil; but at least across the whole history of this planet. It is not something which began with man, although it gets much worse with him. It is there before; it is very difficult, with all that students of natural history give to us, to say there is no evil, nothing contrary to what a perfectly loving God would desire, in the whole of the animal creation.

We very easily exaggerate the suffering of animals because we attribute to them our own appreciation of similar conditions; and with us memory and anticipation, especially in the form of fear, form a very great part of what makes painful or abhorrent those experiences. If they were confined to the moment, a good deal of their terror would be taken away. We have no reason to suppose the animals are haunted by fears. But when all that has been said, surely it remains true that it is very difficult for us to connect up what we know concerning even the animal creation with the thought of the love of God.

This evil that is in the whole world, when it appears at the level of conscious or self-conscious life, is sin. The wonderful myth near the beginning of the Bible describes primitive man as living by rules which he did not understand. They were mere rules, he perceived no principle in them; and it is very important for the understanding of the myth to notice that the Divine Voice later confirms the promise of what the Serpent had said —namely, that by eating of the forbidden tree man would receive the knowledge of good and evil. In a sense he knew it was forbidden, and therefore wrong, but he had not the principle of right and wrong. In his mind the particular commands and prohibitions had not yet been lifted to the level of a principle. It was merely the knowledge, 'You must not do that,' and by breaking the rule man discovered the principle. That is a perfectly familiar experience. Over and over again, as we break some rule which seems rather arbitrary and meaningless, we discover the principle which had dictated it. We set in motion the causes and effects from which we understand, for the first time, why there had ever been that prohibition; then it is too late. The discovery is called the Fall of Man, and in the discovery two things are contained. The first is the actuality of sin; the evil which had previously been impulsive now becomes something known and deliberate. The other is the capacity for relationship with God. We become as God, knowing good and evil, and the capacity for sin and for communion with God are the same capacity. That idea will be perfectly familiar to all of you who have read Aristotle. Many capacities are capacities for opposites. It is the same capacity that leads to both, and what makes us capable of communion or fellowship with God is the same thing that makes anything evil that remains about us definite sin. And let us also recognise that the Fall, which once played so great a part in Christian thought, is a quite plain reality on the basis of evolution, as much as it would be on any other theory, because a deliberately cruel man is certainly worse than an instinctively cruel beast. The fact that the man knows what he is doing, that he is able to compare one course of action with another, and chooses the lower, at once makes that kind of action much worse than the action of a cat satisfying its instincts by playing with a mouse.

The first thing that emerges is a sense of shame—shame in respect of the animal nature. Here again the myth is profoundly right. We have quite deliberately to exercise choice with regard to the kind of life we mean to live, a choice that must go on being repeated over and over again, until a habit or purpose is formed and settled—the choice whether we are going to live according to every impulse that arises in the body, or some other plan which is made possible to us by those elements in our nature, which are human, and human alone. For every human purpose you need some self-control, even for purely selfish ambition of any kind. You must be able to control your impulses so that they do not run away with you; and the first struggle, which all civilised beings have undertaken, and have won some degree of conquest, is the struggle to assert the control of the spirit over the animal nature. Because he is aware that he is called to something higher, in comparison with which the animal nature seems degraded, and because that animal nature is so strong, the first moral impulse in mankind is the impulse of shame. And that conflict with the animal nature goes on through life in one form or another. It is in the assertion of our spiritual character against our animal nature that, more than anywhere else, we have the opportunity of making good our status as citizens of the eternal realm.

From such preliminary considerations we turn to ask how we are to be sure to detect the evil that is in our life. Our moral standard is the mind of Christ. St Paul's definition of sin is 'falling short of the glory of God.' It is quite impossible to estimate the amount of harm done by our habitual limitation of the use of the word 'sin' to deliberate wrong-doing. Everything about us is sin if it is not what God wants it to be. Everything that comes short of the glory of God made manifest in our lives is sin. A great deal of the writings in the New Testament, and a great deal of the language used by Christian people in the history of the Church, is quite unmeaning unless you think of it like that. Now, no doubt all of us can think of acts of quite deliberate wrong about which our consciences ought to be very sensitive, whether they are or not; and it is our duty to look out for these and let them remind us how feeble is our devotion to what we believe to be right. But let us also remember that what is required of us goes a very long way beyond that. It is not enough that a man should always do what he thinks to be his duty; there is an even prior duty to that, namely, that he should think to be his duty what really is his duty. All the deepest sins in the nature of most of us are sins that we have not discovered at all. They are very often associated with something about us with which we are particularly well satisfied. And one of the necessary processes of spiritual development is that we should become aware of one thing after another in our lives, habits of thought and consequent actions with which we have been content hitherto, as entirely alien to the mind of Christ. And that means we cannot rely implicitly upon our consciences.

Conscience is a word used in a great variety of senses; it is really a very vague term, but most people mean by it those spontaneous feelings, sometimes of contentment or approbation, but more often of condemnation or uneasiness, which arise in us with regard to certain sorts of conduct on which we have embarked, or on which we are thinking we may embark; and that sense of condemnation or uneasiness comes as a kind of warning; in a certain sense it may truly be said to be the voice of the Holy Spirit within us, but only in a certain sense. I suppose these spontaneous feelings that arise are the result of the moral training we have had, most of which has been given to us simply by our sharing in the life of our country and our own section in that country, and we have quietly adopted nearly all its standards. We approve these standards, and we shrink away from what defies these standards. In a Christian country these general standards have grown up under the steady influence, but not necessarily the all-controlling influence, of the Spirit of Christ, to which the better part of the population have been referring their own thoughts about right and wrong, and the way in which human life should be conducted; so we should never put them on one side. It is likely that wherever we are thus warned against something we should like to do, the warning is a sound one.

But we are by no means cleared from guilt merely by the fact that our conscience gave no warning, for it may be that with reference to just the kind of action on which we are about to engage, the standard of our country or the section in our country to which we belong is radically false. It would be very rash to say there is any section of English society of which the spontaneously accepted standard of reference is identical with the mind of Christ. We must therefore perpetually criticise these accepted standards and the promptings in our own souls with reference to the mind of Christ, and find out how far it is really justifiable to go in that way—whether, for example, the kind of expenditure upon pleasure which we find to be quite normal among our friends and acquaintances really represents the mind of Christ. We are not all going to find the same answer to these questions, even if we are quite sincere, and we are not going to find any cut-and-dried answer either in the New Testament or in the established books of rules that may have been drawn up at one time or another by wise men in Christ's Church. We are always going to have to think it out for ourselves.

When we put our lives in that way side by side with the mind of Christ, are any of us going to say that the language traditionally put into our mouths is exaggerated? Some people say they do not like to call themselves 'miserable sinners.' If by 'miserable' they mean 'unhappy,' that may be right; they may be perfectly happy sinners. They may be the kind of people who would be happy in hell, because they fitted it. But if by 'miserable' they mean deserving of pity, then are any of us going to deny that we are pitiable sinners? We are indeed sinners, and pitiable sinners.

Our natural tendency is to judge ourselves by the folk round about us. Indeed, the mere pressure of their example and their expectation, and our fear of disappointing that expectation, will go a long way towards holding us up to the commonly accepted standard. For a long way in the spiritual life you have got the world helping you. It is going to help you against the grosser temptations of the flesh, for example. The world is going to help you in your fight against the sins of hatred and malice, because the world likes a kindly and genial nature. But when you come to your struggle with the world, the world is going to be on the wrong side, as when you find that what Christ requires is something which people about you will consider quite foolish and fantastic. It was not only the intelligent Greeks who thought the figure of Christ on the Cross was foolish. Nobody *says* it now, but they think the principle very foolish. When you come to what Christ would ask of you, then, of course, the world will be on the wrong side and your difficulties begin.

Then look round and carry a little further that thought which was before us yesterday; where is it that the greatest evils in the world come from? The greatest actual abominations have come from conscience itself, such as the Inquisition, which was at least instituted on the most profoundly conscientious grounds. When Philip II developed the system and applied the Spanish form of it in the Netherlands, he had one of those convenient consciences which gave him overwhelming moral reason for doing what would, in his opinion, advance the power of the Crown of Spain. Yet he was quite sincere in thinking he was discharging a moral duty to God and man. The great evils that do not come from positive perverted conscience come from the mere fact that the worldly standard is no higher than it is. So long as some millions of people living together are perhaps quite reasonably generous, but always with the limit that their generosity must not seriously impair their own happiness, so that they remain self-centred at the heart, so long there will be these things, or the things that in a different order would correspond to them—wars, slums, and sweated industry. You may do something to bar them out by means of legislation, but, after all, you only get to legislation when people feel that the evil cannot be tolerated at all. Legislation is really the fruit of moral advance, and not the cause of it. The thing that most of us have to become sensitive about is our individual responsibility for the great corporate sins of our nation and civilisation: individual responsibility for corporate sin, because it is our share in it that allows the thing to go on, our share and the share of others just like us. That would not be true perhaps of every evil, but it would have its degree of application almost everywhere. Would you say with regard to prostitution that only those who take advantage of the system for their own indulgence are responsible? Is that true? Why do they take advantage of it? Would they, if all of us maintained the standard about those things which we know to be quite right?

If we only had the common pluck to speak instead of remaining in silence with a silly smirk on our faces when things are said which let the standard down! When the stand is made, we find that most people about us are very glad it has been made; but it needs courage for one to take the lead. Public opinion does not consist of what people think; it consists of that part of what people think which they express. That is what exerts the influence. We have to set ourselves a new standard of what loyalty to the mind of Christ means. And over and over again we shall find ourselves having missed a chance, which will not come back, of making some stand for the cause of Christ which would be a contribution to the abolition of one of the great evils under which the world groans. It is true that for most of our problems there is need for the most careful and searching thought, but no amount of intellectual power will deal with them until people's hearts are right. The only way they can be right is that they should be fully in tune with the mind of Christ. So if this mission leads to nothing else, may it lead to some who have been here making up their minds that they will watch for those chances; so all together we may be doing something really great towards lifting the world's load of evil, which is our sin and the sin of others like us. When you look at that, will you hesitate any longer to say, 'The burden of them is intolerable'? If you do not find it intolerable yet, you ought to find it so. The words represent, not what we are feeling now, but what we ought to feel as disciples of Christ and members of His Body, the Body in which He still carries forth His Cross to Calvary.

John came, and after him Jesus came, saying, 'Change your way of looking at life; the Kingdom of Heaven is at hand.' But we have lowered the term 'repentance' into meaning something not very different from remorse, though, of course, we all are aware that it is not true repentance unless the wrong-doing is abandoned. As the old verse tersely puts it—

> It's not enough to say,
> 'I'm sorry, and repent,'
> And then to go on afterwards
> Just as you always went.

Repentance does not merely mean giving up a bad habit. What it is concerned with is the mind; get a new mind. What mind? The mind of Christ—our standard of reference; learn to look at the world in His way. To repent is to adopt God's viewpoint in place of your own. There need not be any sorrow about it. In itself, far from being sorrowful, it is the most joyful thing in the world, because when you have done it you have adopted the viewpoint of truth itself, and you are in fellowship with God. It means a complete re-valuation of all things we are inclined to think good. The world, as we live in it, is like a shop window in which some mischievous person has got overnight and shifted all the price-labels round so that the cheap things have the high price-labels on them, and the really precious things are priced low. We let ourselves be taken in. Repentance means getting those price-labels back in the right place. The reason our Lord gave for calling one of His disciples 'Satan' was that he thought like a man instead of thinking like God—for that he was called 'Satan.'

No doubt, repentance will often begin in sorrow, because it is our disgust at discovering the kind of people we are that moves us to seek a new attitude of mind. The only thing that matters is getting a new outlook; if sorrow does not lead to that, it is quite useless and wasted. Therefore the first thing necessary for repentance is the vision of God. Do not begin ever considering what is wrong with you without first being quite sure your mind is directed towards the glory of God as it has shone forth in Jesus Christ. In this we must begin by having our minds turned towards God, and the inevitable result of that is always humiliation, as it was for Isaiah when he had heard the song of the Seraphs. 'Woe is me, for I am undone, for I am a man of unclean lips . . . and mine eyes have seen the King, the Lord of Hosts.' In the familiar arrangement of the Holy Communion service in our Prayer Books, there is the same reaction from the same Seraphs' song in the Prayer of Humble Access. You can always know whether you have really attained to any understanding of God by finding out whether you have been humiliated. If not, you have not got there. To get there is the first necessity. As a result of that humiliation we make resolutions of what we will do, and out of the control which that discipline gives us, we get a new appreciation and a fuller vision of God. And the process starts again, and at every stage it is bringing us nearer and nearer to the mind of Christ.

You do not have to wait for Christianity to tell you that an unexamined life is not worth living; that was said by Plato. We must take stock of ourselves. How are you going to do it? There are many aids to self-examination. Some of them are excellent, but some are quite dreadfully bad. I want to suggest how you may know which are the bad ones. If they confront you with a series of questions, all referring to actions, they are bad, because our self-examination must not mainly refer to actions. However searchingly these are treated, the result will be that, with regard to a large number of the questions, you will say, 'Not guilty.' And most times with regard to the ones that remain, either you will decide they do not matter very much, or else you will think they do when they do not. That kind of *ques-*

tionnaire is liable to have one of two bad results; it may make you feel comparatively self-satisfied, and that is the worst state into which any human soul could fall. On the other hand, if, in your eagerness to avoid that fate, you make a great deal of those particular offences with which you find yourselves charged, you may distort your sense of proportion and suppose things to be of primary importance when they are not.

Let your self-examination, as far as possible, concern motives. Confront yourself with the Christian character as it is set out in the Beatitudes or in St Paul's articulation of the Fruit of the Spirit or with some other analysis of the mind of Christ. See how far your character corresponds with this, as exhibited in your actions, feelings, plans and hopes. And do not stifle your conscience by the fallacy that the life of self-sacrifice, being a result of choice, is really as selfish as any other. The height of unselfishness is to *like* giving up your own pleasures for other people's welfare, because then desire itself is sanctified.

Look at your motives. A good many weeks go by in which we do not commit many wrong acts which may come in any catalogue, yet we commit a host of little sins all because our likes and dislikes are out of harmony with the mind of Christ. Remember the motive of repentance is hope; the Kingdom of Heaven is at hand; it always is. If all men were looking at life through the eyes of Christ, feeling for it with His heart, thinking of it with His mind, the Kingdom of Heaven would be come already. The completion of our repentance and the coming of the kingdom are not cause and effect;

they are the same thing viewed from different sides.

What is going to stimulate us to this is not even shame at our own shortcomings; it is going to be the steady practice of that companionship with Jesus Christ which is, after all, the burden of everything I have got to say to you this week. In your prayers think of Him; in making your plans, either for tomorrow or for the future, think of Him. Everywhere be turning back to Him, and 'let this mind be in you which was also in Christ Jesus.'

Let me sing for my well-beloved a song of my beloved touching his vineyard. My well-beloved had a vineyard in a very fruitful hill: and he made a trench about it, and gathered out the stones thereof, and planted it with the choicest vine, and built a tower in the midst of it, and also hewed out a winepress therein: and he looked that it should bring forth grapes, and it brought forth wild grapes. And now, O inhabitants of Jerusalem and men of Judah, judge, I pray you, betwixt me and my vineyard. What could have been done more to my vineyard, that I have not done in it? wherefore, when I looked that it should bring forth grapes, brought it forth wild grapes? And now go to: I will tell you what I will do to my vineyard: I will take away the hedge thereof, and it shall be eaten up; I will break down the fence thereof, and it shall be trodden down: and I will lay it waste; it shall not be pruned nor hoed; but there shall come up briars and thorns: I will also command the clouds that they rain no rain upon it. For the vineyard of the Lord of Hosts is the house of Israel, and the men of Judah his pleasant plant; and he looked for judgement, but behold oppression; for righteousness, but behold a cry.

Now all the publicans and sinners were drawing near unto him for to hear him. And both the Pharisees and the scribes murmured, saying, This man receiveth sinners, and eateth with them. And he spake unto them this parable, saying, What man of you having an hundred sheep, and having lost one of them, doth not leave the ninety and nine in the wilderness, and go after that which is lost, until he find it? And when he hath found it, he layeth it on his shoulders, rejoicing. And when he cometh home, he calleth together his friends and neighbours, saying unto them, Rejoice with me, for I have found my sheep which was lost. I say unto you, that even so there shall be joy in heaven over one sinner that repenteth, more than over ninety and nine righteous persons, which need no repentance. Or what woman having ten pieces of silver, if she lose one piece, doth not light a lamp, and sweep diligently until she find it? And when she hath found it, she calleth together her friends and neighbours, saying, Rejoice with me, for I have found the piece which I had lost. Even so, I say unto you, there is joy in the presence of the angels of God over one sinner that repenteth.

Come unto me, all ye that labour and are heavy laden, and I will give you rest. Take my yoke upon you and learn of me; for I am meek and lowly in heart: and ye shall find rest in your souls. For my yoke is easy and my burden is light.

For God hath shut up all unto disobedience, that he might have mercy upon all. O the depth of the riches both of the wisdom and the knowledge of God! how unsearchable are his judgements, and his ways past tracing out! For who hath known the mind of the Lord? or who hath been his counsellor? or who hath first given to him, and it shall be recompensed unto him again? For of him, and through him, and unto him, are all things. To him be the glory for ever. Amen.

THE MEANING OF THE CRUCIFIXION

'"LET there be light"; and there was light.' 'And He
was parted from them about a stone's cast; and He
kneeled down and prayed, saying, Father, if Thou be
willing, remove this cup from Me; nevertheless not My
will, but Thine be done ... And being in an agony He
prayed more earnestly; and His sweat was, as it were,
great drops of blood falling down upon the ground.'

In those two quotations there is depicted the difference
for God between creating the universe with all its
millions of stars, and the making of a selfish soul into
a loving one. To create was easy; the will of God pro-
duces its own fulfilment; no effort there. '"Let there
be light"; and there was light.' But to convert a heart
like our hearts from the self-centredness which is natural
to them into the love which is God's own nature, which
they must reach if they are to be in fellowship with Him
—that costs the agony and the bloody sweat and the
death upon the Cross.

Remember, first, its place in the story. At Cæsarea
Philippi He had been recognised by one of those He
had chosen to be with Him, and the rest had acquiesced
at least in the recognition. From that moment they are
the followers of a Messiah. What was universally expected of the Messiah was that He should found the
Kingdom of God; one of the most familiar images was

that of a triumphal procession which He would lead, and He warns them what it would be like. There is going to be a triumphal procession, He says, but it will not look like one. What it will look like is a gang of condemned criminals following their Leader to a place of execution. 'If any man would come after Me, let him take up his cross and follow Me.' Crucifixion was a thing much too common in that time and place for anyone to use it as an easy metaphor for the little troubles of daily life. Those words must be taken in solemn earnest.

The moment He has been recognised, and after the Transfiguration, in which His acceptance of the claim, so to speak, is ratified, and even more than ratified, for it is the proclamation of something more than Messiahship, He begins the new teaching that the thing He will do to make good His Messiahship is to suffer. And at once He starts for Jerusalem. It has all been carefully planned; there is the man there with whom the password has been agreed, so that when the disciples ask for the ass he will give him: 'The Lord hath need of him.' It is all thought out. He deliberately fulfils Zechariah's prophecy; thereby he declares the sort of Messiah. He is going to be, for the ass is the beast upon which great officers rode when they came peacefully, while the horse represented conquest and force. And closely connected in the prophecy are the words: 'He shall speak peace unto the nations.' But there could be no doubt that He was fulfilling the prophecy; and it was very difficult for the authorities at Jerusalem to ignore the claim that He was making; it was difficult to ignore the claim of the triumphal entry. He then makes their position quite impossible unless they are prepared to accept Him, by the cleansing of the Temple, asserting His authority in a place where only the authority of the high priests should be recognised, and abolishing vested interests which had the sanction, if not of the Law, at least of long custom. They are bound to act. And then, in a way we shall be thinking of on Saturday, with equal care He arranges for the privacy He needs for the Last Supper, and proceeds from it to the same place to which He had gone every evening, so that the arrest may be a certainty. As He stands before them and is challenged with the claim He has openly made, He declares that the Parousia is begun: 'From this moment there shall be the Son of Man seated on the right hand of power.' And so it has been. From that moment He has put forth His power over the world in a perpetually increasing control of men's hearts and wills, and the focal source of that power is the Cross.

We are not reading a record only of something that happened long ago; we are looking on the picture of God as He eternally is, 'The Word was made flesh and we beheld His glory,' and we behold it still. We see the Love which is the innermost nature of God confronted with its own rejection and how it deals with the situation; this rejection is the ultimate assertion of selfishness itself —its utmost and its worst; and the thing it achieves is the source of all that is best in the experience of men from then until now. By the way in which He bore it He turns the devil's worst into God's best. But the fact is the same fact; it is that which we are trying to understand.

All real thought about the Atonement, about the meaning of the Cross of Christ, must of course start from the love of God. There have been some crude kinds of statement suggesting that it starts with His anger, which needs to be appeased. You must never start from there. 'God so loved the world, that He gave His only begotten Son.' 'God commendeth His love towards us in that while we were yet sinners, Christ died.' It does not begin with His anger; it begins with His love, the love that must desire always to restore the old relationship we have broken, or lead us into the true relationship of children to their Father upon which we have never entered.

At the heart of the Gospel is the promise of free forgiveness on condition of repentance, of which the exquisite expression is the parable of the Prodigal Son; and yet how can God forgive without demoralising us and even without abandoning His own character of perfect holiness? It is one of the charges brought by Hinduism and Buddhism against Christianity that the doctrine of forgiveness must be immoral. They urge that there is a purer justice in their doctrine of Karma—the doctrine that through successive incarnations, we build up progressively a character which, at every stage, suffers precisely that which is appropriate, and which may lead to fellowship with such gods as exist, or to passing out into the state of peace beyond understanding which is called Nirvana.

Is it true that forgiveness must be immoral? Well, forgiveness, as men often understand the word, if it comes all by itself, is likely to be immoral. What would be

immoral on God's part, and demoralising to us, would
be that He should say to us concerning all our selfishness
and nastiness, 'Oh, never mind; come along; let us still
be friends.' 'He's a good fellow and 'twill all be well.'
That kind of attitude is demoralising; and God could
not safely make known the love which always yearns
to forgive, and the forgiveness which the love offers
to repentance, unless at the same time He showed us
what our selfishness had all the while been meaning to
Him. If it were merely that from the undisturbed peace
of the Heaven whence He looks down on earth, He
were to say, 'Never mind,' we could no longer worship
Him. He would be below the level of our own consciences. But no one who has received his pardon from the
lips of Christ on the Cross is going to think that God
says 'Never mind,' or that He does not Himself mind.
That is how He minds. That is the eternal picture of
what the self-centredness of the men of that generation,
and of all others, and of our own, means to God. And
because of that, because He has displayed what it means
to Him, He can pronounce the words of pardon that
welcome us back into intimacy without any damage to
our conscience, but rather making our consciences much
more sensitive than they were before.

There is the first great function of the Cross in the
economy of the Divine purpose in creation and redemption. It makes righteous the forgiving love of God. And
if you read carefully the third chapter of the Epistle to
the Romans you will see that, though using the termino-
logy of a period not our own, this is what St Paul is
concerned about. Can this forgiving love of God be

perfectly righteous, or, if He is perfectly righteous, can He show forgiving love? Yes, He can, for He sets forth Christ in His Blood as the propitiation. But the word translated 'propitiation' also means 'mercy seat'—the meeting-place of God's holy love and man's sin. And the blood of Christ is His life offered in sacrifice to the cause of the Kingdom of God. How truly that Life was offered to God and for God's Kingdom we shall be considering on Saturday.

Then we turn from God's side to our own. 'You shall be forgiven if you repent.' But how can I repent; I only do wrong things because I like them; I cannot stop liking them because you tell me not to like them any more; I can only stop liking them if I become a new kind of person or I see them in some new perspective. It is no use to tell a man he will be forgiven if he will repent, unless you tell him how to repent. As Coleridge truly said, the supreme merit of the Gospel is not that it promises forgiveness to those who repent, but that it promises repentance to those who sin, if only they will truly put their faith into practice, or, in other words, if, whenever they are conscious of failing in any way to correspond to the will of the perfect love of God, they will realise what their failure means to Him. If we will recall Christ in Gethsemane, Christ upon the Cross, as the manifestation of what our failure means to God, there is no sin in our lives so dear to us, but we shall long to be rid of it just in the degree in which we make that picture real and vivid in ourselves, and constantly dwell upon it. So the second great function of the Cross is to enable us to qualify to receive the forgiveness which

God always yearns to offer; it makes it possible for Him to give and for us to receive.

Only what is forgiveness? I have already used the phrase which seems best to represent it; but we are liable to have an altogether unworthy notion of forgiveness because our conception of God as our Father is so dim. We do not really think of Him as loving with a father's love; still less do we love Him as His children. Therefore our minds are full of dreadful pictures drawn from the law-courts; people even talk about the great scene which pictures the gathering up of human history as a great assize. But the prisoner in the dock has no personal relationship to the judge upon the bench; he does not have to think what pain his misconduct has caused to the judge; all he thinks about is what the judge is going to do to him. It is a poor kind of family life in which that is what the child thinks about the father when the child has given offence. Once there is love, forgiveness does not mean remission of penalty. Penalty does not come in. Forgiveness means restoration to intimacy. That is what is made possible for us. If we, as individuals, have to say that never in our experience can we look back on a time when we were intimate with God, let us remember we are part of the great human race, and we enter upon this inheritance of self-centredness. With us personally it may not be restoration; but that is what forgiveness is—the cancelling of the alienation and the bringing us into true fellowship and communion.

When we have that quite clearly in our minds we may dispense once and for all with those notions which have troubled men, that what our Lord bore was the penalty that was really due to our sins. The truth that lay behind it surely was that, by His suffering, our Lord did make it possible for us to avoid suffering continual alienation from God and the consequences of this; and therefore, in a sense, His suffering is substituted for ours; but it is not a transferred penalty: it is something in the nature of a price paid; it is something which He gave, by means of which we are set free. It is a real redemption; but what He is concerned with all the time is delivering us, not from the consequences of sin, but from sin; and the centre of sin is self. So He is delivering us out of self-centredness into a life that finds its centre in God.

As we study the method of our Lord in dealing with men, we find He is prepared to use vehemence, and even violence, of speech and denunciation, for breaking up the self-complacency that hinders the entrance of His love's appeal. His denunciation seems to be reserved for those who are self-satisfied, and therefore for those who are comparatively virtuous. For it is only they who can be satisfied. His aim is to draw you into the true fellowship of love, which means that your own life becomes filled with it and you desire rather to serve than to gain. And you can refuse. I am not going to say, during this week, anything about the bewildering subject of the ultimate fate of the soul which refuses the love of God. On the one side it seems clear that we have the power to refuse, and He will not override it; on the other side there are those who say that, in respect of a soul that finally rejects His love, Almighty God has failed; and that is inconceivable. There, I think, we must leave it, recognising that it is the kind of problem which peculiarly belongs to the eternal world, and is therefore not likely to be open to complete solution here. But one thing we can say with confidence: everlasting torment is to be ruled out. If men had not imported the Greek and unbiblical notion of the natural indestructibility of the individual soul, and then read the New Testament with that already in their minds, they would have drawn from it a belief, not in everlasting torment, but in anni-hilation. It is the fire that is called æonian, not the life cast into it. But what the New Testament does most surely teach is the reality of 'abiding consequences' of all we do.

It is no part of the Gospel to try to deliver men by fear. Fear is the most self-centred of all emotions, and the use of it as a constant moral appeal can only make us more self-centred, and therefore must defeat the very object it is desired to attain. The way of eternal love is the way of the Cross.

Some of you are familiar, I expect, with the wonder-ful novel of Dostoevsky, in which occurs the fable of the Grand Inquisitor. I will not tell it at full length, but compress it as follows. In the days of the Inquisition, the fable runs, our Lord returned to earth and visited a city where it was at work. As He moved about, men forgot their cares and sorrows, and all was joy and happiness. He healed the sick folk as of old, and, meeting with a funeral procession, where a widow was mourning her only son, He stopped the procession and restored the dead boy to life and to his mother. That was in the cathedral square; and at that moment, through the great doors of the cathedral, came out the Grand Inquisitor, an old man, ninety years of age, clad, not in the gorgeous cardinal's robe (in which on the previous day he had condemned a score of heretics to the stake), but in a plain cassock, with two guards in attendance. He saw what was done, and, turning to the guards, he said, 'Arrest Him.' They obeyed, and the Inquisitor sent his Prisoner to the dungeon.

That night the Grand Inquisitor visited his Prisoner, and to all he said the Prisoner made no reply. 'I know why Thou art come,' said the Inquisitor; 'Thou art come to repeat Thy great mistake in the wilderness and to spoil our work. What did the great and wise Spirit offer Thee there? Just the three things by which men may be controlled: Bread, and Authority, and Mystery. He bade Thee take bread as the instrument of Thy work; men will follow one who gives them bread. But Thou wouldest not; men were to follow Thee out of love and devotion, or not at all. We have had to correct Thy work, or there would be few to follow Thee. He bade Thee assume authority; men will obey one who rewards the obedient and punishes the disobedient. But Thou wouldest not; men were to obey Thee out of love and devotion, or not at all. We have had to correct Thy work, or there would be few to obey Thee. He bade Thee show some marvel that men might be astounded, and believe; they will believe in one who is wrapped in mystery. But Thou wouldest not; men were to believe in Thee out of love and devotion, or not at all. We have had to correct Thy work, or there would be few to believe on Thee. And now Thou art come to repeat Thy great mistake and spoil our work; but it shall not be, for tomorrow I shall burn Thee.'

The Inquisitor ceased; and still the Prisoner made no reply, but rose from where He sat, and crossed the cell, and kissed the old man on his bloodless lips. Then the Inquisitor opened the door; 'Go,' he said. The Prisoner passed out into the night, and was not seen again.

And the old man? That kiss burned in his heart, but he did not alter his opinion or practice.

Are we going to alter ours?

> Love so amazing, so divine,
> Demands my soul, my life, my all.

If that is the demand it makes—soul, life, all—what is our response to the demand? How do we show we are responding? By giving that for which it makes appeal: love exhibited in repentance, which we saw yesterday means the taking of His mind in place of our own, the mind of love in place of our selfish mind. He gave us the parable of the Prodigal Son, and that means that forgiveness is offered to our repentance, and our repentance is its proper counterpart. But when He was not speaking in parables, He picked out one part of repentance and always laid His emphasis there; it was that we, too, should be forgiving. You will remember how impossible it is to exaggerate the emphasis He lays on that. And the reason is plain enough; it is the supreme test. Anyone can love his friends; anyone can love people who are kind to him; the test is 'Love your enemies.' That is forgiveness. Treat your enemies as if they were your friends. That is the great test of whether your heart is in tune with God; for that is what God Himself does. He sends His rain on the just and the unjust, and we are to be perfect in the same way that our Heavenly Father is perfect—that is, with the perfection of undiscriminating love.

I do not suppose many of you are conscious of having any definite enemies; one's life in this University is mainly a life of good fellowship, and those who are not congenial to us we need not meet with very much. So there is not much friction, and there is hardly any society in the world more free from real hatreds. Therefore it is not easy to find outstanding opportunities for practising this great virtue of forgiveness. But there are plenty of little ones, and the little ones test us more searchingly because there is nothing heroic about them. It is always easier to do one big heroic thing than a thousand little, obscure things; and that is what it has got to be with most of us. We can see why He insists on this so much. Whether you look to our relationship to God or our relationship to man, we are children in God's family, and, God having let us know the love in His heart, we ask to be received into the home that we had left; and He says, 'Yes, but can you be friends with so and so? I am ready to have you, but I cannot have you if you are going to quarrel with him all day.' We may never approach God at all except as children in His family. This forgiveness is part of repentance; but there is all the difference in the world between coming to Him and saying, 'I am sorry; I won't do it again; will you have me back?' and saying, 'I think I can get rid, under the inspiration of the love You have shown, of all the little resentments and spites in my heart. May I come back?' It is the second that He requires; He says it over and over again; and He puts it in the prayer He taught us. If we do not forgive, then even though He offers forgiveness we are not receiving it. Fellowship with Him means that we become loving; and that will show itself in our being forgiving. And if we do not become forgiving, then, even though He offers His love, we are shutting it out. It is not that our forgiveness is on the scale of His. You remember the parable of the unforgiving servant. The debt which the servant owed to his lord was about two and a half million pounds. When he went up and said, 'Have patience with me, and I will pay thee all,' he was making a promise he could never fulfil; yet the lord forgave him the debt. He then met a fellow-servant who owed him about five pounds, and who made the same request, and might hope to keep his promise; but that plea was not granted. Then the servant was told he had shut away from himself the forgiveness that had been offered to him because his heart was not capable of receiving it. Intimacy with God means becoming filled with love towards everyone —love which means the desire to do what will be good for them and not what will be good or pleasant for us. You see how far that carries us up in the moral struggle against all the disreputable sins.

But it was respectable people who crucified Christ, people of well-established traditions; and they crucified Him because He asked of them something that went beyond their tradition. That is the eternal picture of the relationship, part conflict, but more profoundly the perpetual victory of love over the selfishness in our hearts, which is the triumph of the Gospel. There is more love in the world now than there was. The cause goes forward slowly and with difficulty; but it goes forward. There is no doubt about it. 'The action of Christ who is risen,' said Acton, 'upon mankind whom He has redeemed, fails not, but increases.' Christ is winning; and He asks us to join His victorious host as members of His army. The terms of the invitation are familiar: If any man will come after Me, let him deny himself (not think about himself in this world or any other world) and take up his cross (be ready for just anything) and follow Me.

For hereunto were ye called; because Christ also suffered for you, leaving you an example, that ye should follow his steps: who did no sin, neither was guile found in his mouth: who, when he was reviled, reviled not again; when he suffered, threatened not; but committed himself to him that judgeth righteously; who his own self bare our sins in his body on the tree, that we, having died unto sins, might live unto righteousness; by whose stripes ye were healed. For ye were going astray like sheep; but are now returned unto the Shepherd and Bishop of your souls.

Wherefore if any man is in Christ, there is a new creation: the old things are passed away; behold, they are become new. But all things are of God, who reconciled us to himself through Christ, and gave unto us the ministry of reconciliation; to wit, that God was in Christ reconciling the world unto himself, not reckoning unto them their trespasses, and having committed unto us the word of reconciliation. We are ambassadors therefore on behalf of Christ, as though God were entreating by us: we beseech you on behalf of Christ, be ye reconciled to God.

Having therefore, brethren, boldness to enter into the holy place by the blood of Jesus, by the way which he dedicated for us, a new and living way, through the veil, that is to say, his flesh; and having a great priest over the house of God; let us draw near with a true heart in fulness of faith, having our hearts sprinkled from an evil conscience, and our body washed with pure water.

Unto him that loveth us, and loosed us from our sins by his blood; and he made us to be a kingdom, to be priests unto his God and Father; to him be the glory and the dominion for ever and ever. Amen.

6

THE HOLY SPIRIT IN LIFE

THIS evening our subject is the Holy Spirit. We often hear it said that this is a peculiarly difficult and remote part of Christian belief. I have even heard clergymen say that they find Whit Sunday the hardest of all the Church festivals to preach upon. If so, I think it shows, among other things, that we very easily let our distinctively religious thought get detached in a very disastrous fashion from our ordinary thought, because, in plain point of fact, the Holy Spirit is the Person in the Trinity with whom we are most constantly in conscious contact.

You may begin at either end. Let us begin with the thought of the steady impulse towards advance and progress which science discloses to us in the evolutionary series of developments which have apparently taken place in the history of this planet. Science does not in the least know why this process goes forward at all; it can only trace out some of the laws in accordance with which it moves forward. The different schools of biology deal in different ways with the 'unknown factor,' but for all of them there is an 'unknown factor.' If the initiation of a new species always is some spontaneous variation, what is the word 'spontaneous' except a confession of ignorance? What caused it to happen? Here is the whole process moving steadily forward in a transformation, up to date, for the most part out of chaos into order.

It is quite true that the prospect held out before us as
regards the solar system and the stellar universe is something like a reversion to chaos again; but, at any rate,
up to date and culminating in life as a vehicle of intelligent purpose and spiritual devotion, there has been
an advance from chaos to order. If we are going to
speak in the language of the imagination about it, can
we do better than to say, 'the earth was waste and void,
and darkness was on the face of the deep; and the Spirit
of God was brooding upon the face of the waters'? All
that process, for one who believes in God as the Creator
of the world, who sustains it and guides it according
to His own will, who is the origin of the laws it un-
failingly obeys—all that process is the work of the Spirit
of God in the universe.

When you come to human history it is still the same,
the creation of ever more perfect order, whether you
think of the individual or of society. In the individual
there are to begin with a number of impulses which seem
to have very little relation to one another, which it is
very hard indeed to co-ordinate, and every one of which
is in its own nature apparently insatiable. It will pursue
its appropriate end so long as there is any stimulus to
such pursuit in its environment; and spiritual development largely consists in bringing order into that which
is chaos. The Greeks took sculpture as an illustration of
this process. The sculptor takes a shapeless block of
marble. Of course, in one sense it has a shape; but this
is æsthetically irrelevant; its surfaces might as well be
anywhere else as where they are; it is infinite in the bad
sense—indeterminate. The sculptor reduces it within

bounds, and thereby endues it with significance; and that for them was an analogy, and a striking analogy, to what has to be done with the initial endowment of the nature of any human individual. It has to be brought within bounds, and every part of it made to confine itself within its appropriate proportions; and so significance is given to the whole life and to every part of it.

The whole process of social and civic development is the parallel growth of two things: the richness of individual personality with completeness of social intercourse. The development of personality in fellowship is no bad definition of what we mean by progress. All this we find going on from stage to stage, and, broadly speaking, there is no doubt about the advance. Again, the believer in God has no doubt at all that the impulse moving the whole world forward is the Spirit of God. All the great theologians have always said that the love wherewith a man loves God or his neighbour is the Holy Ghost. It is not the *work* of the Holy Ghost only, it *is* the Holy Ghost. It is God, the supreme, eternal, universal Spirit at work in the hearts of His creatures; and that involves a consequence to which we must come back.

And above all, it is the Holy Spirit who is the Author of every transcendent claim, whence-soever it may come. Whenever a man feels called upon to neglect his natural interests or his animal desires in the service of any sort of ideal whatsoever, there you have the movement of the Holy Spirit. The man of course may himself interpret it in many ways; he may not understand the source of the urge within him, and may connect it up quite wrongly with all sorts of other things; but the man who believes in God will have no doubt that the obligation of which an artist is conscious, to devote himself to the highest beauty he can conceive, is the work of the Holy Spirit in his soul. When the man of science puts aside all other considerations except the pursuit of truth, that is again the activity of the Holy Spirit. And most conspicuously in all those relationships between men which are studied in the science of ethics, the sense of obligation—the sense that there are some things which, if the opportunity comes, we must do, and that there are certain other things which, whatever the advantage to be derived from them, we must on no account do—this is the Holy Spirit.

But if that were all we had to say, there would apparently be no particular distinction to be drawn between the Holy Spirit and what we spoke of the other day as the Word of God; and here we come to a point of the very greatest practical importance. All the Apostles of our Lord spoke of God distinctively as the Holy Spirit, as they experienced the new power which God obtained over the hearts of men by the manifestation of His love in a human life which they could understand in the Person of Jesus Christ. As you read the New Testament you have no doubt at all about that; they felt the whole relationship had been altered. Previously it had been the relationship of master and slave; God gave His commands and we were to obey them. If we did we should be rewarded, if we failed we should be punished. In the highest flights of Old Testament prophecy and poetry you find something more than this, and yet it remains basic; in the New Testament it is basic no longer. We do not receive the spirit of slavery; we receive the spirit of adoption whereby we speak of God as Father, and that, too, with the special note of tender intimacy which had been imparted into the word as our Lord uttered it: Abba, Father. This new power could only come when men received and were able to respond to the knowledge of God that is given in Christ; and that could not be given except in the fashion of a human life, because nothing else would really exhibit it to human minds and hearts. It was in order that this power might come, you may say, that our Lord ever came Himself at all; and it was for that He went away. Think how strange it must have seemed to the disciples when He said, 'It is expedient for you that I go away.' He does not say, 'The time is bound to come when we must part: therefore you must be prepared.' He says, 'It is a good thing for you that it should come.' Why? Because 'If I go not away the Comforter will not come unto you: but if I depart I will send Him unto you.' What happened to the faith of the Apostles who had been relying on our Lord as a Person by their side to whom they could turn? It was genuine enough; it was loyal; but it was not deep enough, and in the great crisis it went to pieces. 'All the disciples forsook Him and fled.' And a few weeks later these same people became the nucleus of what is at the lowest the most remarkable of the associations of mankind, the Christian Church. What had happened to those Galilean fishermen who, in the great crisis, had run away, that they should stand up and talk to the high priests as they do in the Acts? It was this: they were no longer relying on a Lord who was an external Presence to them, but One who had returned to them, who dwelt in their hearts, the very breath of their lives. Our Lord breathed on them and said, 'Receive the Holy Breath.' He would be no longer there to work for them; but He would be there at work within them.

The Holy Spirit, as Christians know Him, is not merely the diffused power of God discoverable everywhere in the universe, but is first and foremost the special and distinctive influence which God exerts over our souls as we respond to His love in the human life of Christ. And the difference is fundamentally this; that now, instead of having regulations which we are to obey, deliberately considering how they apply, we have, in the degree in which we dwell in Christ's companionship, a desire to do the things that please God. The great conflict in the Gospels is between our Lord and the Pharisees, and it is the conflict between the religion of the Spirit and the religion of a code. Those Pharisees were the heirs of the greatest religious tradition then extant in the world; and they were not unworthy heirs. They and their sons, in the great siege of Jerusalem forty years after the Crucifixion, were going to show a heroism worthy of their ancestors. But if you make your religion into any form of code, so that it consists of regulations, two bad things are going to happen. You are going to frighten off the people who know they cannot keep your code. If all you have for them is commands to obey, they will shrug their shoulders and go off, and so you fail to help those who need help most. It is bad for those who cannot keep the code; but it is much worse for those who can; for they get self-satisfied. In the parable of the Pharisee and the publican the whole point is that the Pharisee

was a much better man than the publican; only he was
not going to become any better than he was that day
unless something came to break up his self-complacency;
whereas the publican was discontented and therefore
might grow; with eternity before him he might come
right home at last.

This is to be the aim of our practice of religion: not
merely that we should know more fully what the Will
of God is, but that we should strengthen within ourselves the perpetual desire to do what pleases Him. 'Thou
shalt love the Lord thy God.' With men, love means that
you like being with them, are glad when you do what
pleases them, and sorry when you do what pains them.
The love of God means just that. And when you love,
you do not laboriously think out and perform the will
of the beloved; you wish to please him, and largely, at
least, trust to your spontaneous sense of what will do
this. That may begin to be true and become increasingly
true of our service of God, just in the degree in which
we genuinely set ourselves to live in the constant companionship of our Lord.

When we have learned the nature and character of
the Holy Spirit in this way, we can afterwards trace His
operation in the same character over the whole field of
nature and history. But you must not begin with nature
and history; you must begin with Jesus Christ. The way
to find His power in your heart is to be perpetually
turning your eyes towards the objective revelation there
given on the stage of history. Jesus is not only the revelation of the Spirit; He is the source of that Spirit to us.
Into our lives, as in the Being of the Godhead, the Holy

Spirit proceeds not only from the Father, but from the Father through the Son.

This power which develops in our hearts is the response which God calls out from our hearts by the revelation given in His Son, and you cannot know the power of the Holy Spirit in its fullness except by the companionship of Jesus Christ.

For this reason it is said of Him that He sanctifies 'all the elect people of God.' The elect are those to whom, through no merit of their own, great opportunities of influence or service have come. The greatest of all the opportunities there is, or ever can be, in the world is to know the character of God, the ultimate reality upon whose Will everything depends; and so to know it that our hearts are called out in sympathy so that we not only do His Will thinking it must be sensible to do what He wants, but that we want to do it. That will to do it, in the heart of man, that is the Holy Spirit. His claim is to pervade and control all life.

People sometimes say, when they are excusing themselves for a departure from some rule, that they do not govern their lives by the letter but by the spirit. What they mean, of course, is that they break their rules whenever they feel inclined. But the spirit is going to be much more exacting than the letter. We can see St Peter in the Gospel trying to get a nice Pharisaic rule about that duty of forgiveness on which our Lord laid such terrifying stress. He knows it must be a stiff rule; but he would like to know what he must aim at and when he may stop. We are apt to say, 'I have befriended so and so three times over, and I do not think anyone can expect me to do any more.' And we like our friends to say, 'No, my dear, I do not think they can.' St Peter knows three times will not be enough. Will seven times do? No; four hundred and ninety; more times than it is conceivable that one man should injure another. Why? It means that there is no rule about it; but if there is the spirit of God in your heart you will want to forgive him every time; the question will not arise.

Now there is a great need in most of us for the use of more rules in our lives than we are in fact using, but these rules must be our servants, not our masters. They are the ways in which we take steps to secure that the increasingly predominant power in our lives is the power of the Holy Spirit, the Spirit of the Eternal God welling up in our hearts in answer to the revelation of the same Eternal God revealed in Jesus Christ; for it is one God in all His manifestations. But it is by the use we make of the revelation God has given us that we are able to bring ourselves under the influence of the Spirit. So there is the secret of finding the Holy Spirit in life; it is the companionship with Christ, constant and perpetual, in worship, in all the daily tasks of life as we try perpetually to refer to Him our aspirations and ambitions, and by His mind to check all our thoughts, feelings and desires, and in the service of the kingdom which He came to found, and for which He calls on us to be His fellow-workers in preparing.

'The promised day of God' is always ready to come on two conditions. First, that the Gospel is made known to the world, and, secondly, that men continually act upon their belief in it. 'Repent, for the Kingdom of Heaven is at hand.' Our trouble is twofold. It is partly a total neglect of the Gospel, and partly the failure of those who nominally accept it, to base their practice upon it. They neglect the opportunities which exist, such as opportunities of public worship: particularly those who, when they go, expect to have everything done for them and to be carried along on a tide which is generated by those responsible for the ordering of that worship.

If you go to church, for example, only to stand there while somebody else sings hymns, and kneel there—or more probably, not kneel, but adopt that astonishingly uncomfortable and completely undevotional attitude which is so familiar—while someone says prayers, how can you expect it to have any effect on you except a deadening one? But if we open our hearts to the reality that is there, and, if there seems to be not much reality, at least bring some of our own, then we shall begin to live up to our profession, which is to follow our Saviour Christ and be made like unto Him.

You cannot make yourself like Him; but He can make you like Himself. And here we come to what I suppose is one of the deepest facts about our nature. We are so constituted that we may be described as possessing a will. That is to say, our personalities have certain goals before them or certain principles accepted by them, by which they are guided even if there are many obstacles to hamper the guidance. And this determination of our personality, which we call 'will,' is capable of regulating our actions to a certain extent.

We ought to exercise our wills a good deal more than we do, and make ourselves worth more than we are; but there is something deeper than that to be touched. The root trouble with us is that our wills themselves are not in harmony with God's, or at the very best are in incomplete and imperfect harmony with God's. That is something which you cannot alter by yourself. Whatever the freedom of the will may mean, it is sheer nonsense if it means that a selfish man can make himself unselfish. What, then, can you do about it? You can make what is far the most important choice anybody ever has to make at all; that is the choice of those influences by which you deliberately submit yourself to be moulded. You can, in your better moments, determine that there shall no day pass in which you do not spend so much time in deliberate contemplation of Jesus Christ, and in the desire to be made like Him so far as you are able to feel the desire. And gradually, just as through the intimacy with a great masterpiece of art your appreciation of it is quickened, so you will become more sensitive to the greatness of that character.

It is here that we want our rules—rules about our prayers, rules about our worship, about our use of the Holy Communion, of which we shall be thinking to-morrow. You want rules about these things, because if you leave yourself to drift, you always drift the wrong way. You do not drift into public worship; you do not drift into the service of Holy Communion. You let it go by, unless you make up your mind to use it; and you make your use of it comparatively futile unless you think out in advance how you will go, and what your prepara-

tion shall be. We want rules; different people want
different rules no doubt, but we all of us want rules.
We shall drift into futility unless we have rules; we
rightly break our rules when we are convinced that we
can serve God better by breaking them, but it must
be because we are serving God better and not pleasing
ourselves better.

There is the first thing—the bringing of the inner life
under the control of the Holy Spirit by the perpetual
discipline which brings us back, day by day, to the
remembrance and companionship of Jesus Christ. Upon
that everything else depends, for if the inward life is not
sound you cannot do much with the outer. More particularly as concerning the influence you exert on other
people—in many walks of life your highest responsibility
—everything will turn on the reality of the interior
communion of your soul with Jesus Christ. Out of that
will spring the power of the Holy Spirit in your life;
and it will work out in the lives of those for whom, in
different measures, you are responsible.

Let us also seek for the movements of the Spirit in
the world about us, and take our share in them. There
is no difficulty in finding the movements of the Spirit,
because wherever the fruits of the Spirit are, there is He.
If you find something going forward which promotes
true fellowship, there you know the Holy Spirit is at
work, and you may come yourself increasingly under
His influence by taking your share there. It may be that
those with whom you join are not themselves Christians,
and do not recognise the power that is moving them for
what it is. Never mind that. You may have the oppor-

tunity of helping them to understand it, to their ines-
timable gain. But if you cannot, do not let that hinder
your co-operation; for it still is the work of the Holy
Spirit. And you will come to realise that this Spirit by
which you are moved, which is the Spirit of Christ, is
always leading you to greater fullness of life. Here we
find the clue to one of those problems we were speaking
of earlier, and about which I said that there is no general
solution, but each must find the solution for himself:
namely, the degree in which it is right for any individual
to abandon opportunities of what seem like self-realisation in order to do service of some kind or another to
other people, where the exercise of our special talents
may perhaps bring little benefit. There is this to help
us. If the true life of man whereby he fulfils his destiny
of fellowship with God is the life of Jesus Christ, then
true self-realisation must always consist very largely of
self-sacrifice. If there is no sacrifice in a life, the self you
are realising cannot be your true self, but only some
conventional self which you have formed in your mind
and like to dwell upon. Real self-realisation will always
include self-sacrifice; and there is no self-sacrifice so
thorough-going that it cannot be the completest self-
realisation. The greatest thing that can happen to any
human soul is to become utterly filled with love; and
self-sacrifice is love's natural expression. There can be
no sacrifice so great that it may not be the true realisation
of the true self.

But in this life of companionship with Christ which
we secure by discipline, we find also the surest promise
that we shall discover, each of us our own vocation.

And here I turn once more to a theme I have already spoken of; that the duty of any one of us is—so far as we may—to find out what God requires of us, and to do it as the work which God has given us. Whatever the work you do for your living, it must be a form of service of some kind, for no one will pay you for your work if he does not want it done. What makes all the difference is what you are thinking of first and foremost, as you consider the spirit and temper in which you carry out your work. Is it your livelihood or is it God's service? The work in itself is both. But which do you think of first? Nothing would bring nearer the promised day of God than that all Christian people should enter on their profession in the spirit of those who regard it as their chief sphere of serving God. And if we are to attain to that, we come back to the thing I have spoken of so often that it must seem I have no other thought in my mind—the companionship of Christ, out of which springs that Divine power in our hearts, which is our answer to it.

Over and over again we are filled with despair because our love is so cold and feeble. No; it is not feeble; it is almighty; for it is God the Holy Ghost, waiting until we give Him opportunity. For here, as always, He will force nothing on us. But the strength He gives, even to love Him, is always sufficient if we try to obey His command, relying not on our own power, but on His— His Spirit, who is His very Self at work within our souls.

If ye love me, ye will keep my commandments. And I will pray the Father and he shall give you another Comforter, that he may be with you for ever, even the Spirit of truth: whom the world cannot receive; for it beholdeth him not, neither knoweth him: ye know him; for he abideth with you, and shall be in you. I will not leave you desolate: I will come unto you. Yet a little while, and the world beholdeth me no more; but ye behold me: because I live, ye shall live also. In that day ye shall know that I am in my Father, and ye in me, and I in you.

For as many as are led by the spirit of God, these are the sons of God. For ye received not the spirit of bondage again unto fear; but ye received the spirit of adoption, whereby we cry, Abba, Father. The Spirit himself beareth witness with our spirit, that we are children of God: and if children, then heirs; heirs of God, and joint-heirs with Christ; if so be that we suffer with him, that we may be also glorified with him.

For I reckon that the sufferings of this present time are not worthy to be compared with the glory which shall be revealed to us-ward. For the earnest expectation of the creation waiteth for the revealing of the sons of God. For the creation was subjected to vanity, not of its own will, but by reason of him who subjected it, in hope that the creation itself also shall be delivered from the bondage of corruption into the liberty of the glory of the children of God. For we know that the whole creation groaneth and travaileth in pain together until now. And not only so, but ourselves also, which have the firstfruits of the Spirit, even we ourselves groan within ourselves, waiting for our adoption, to wit, the redemption of our body. For by hope were we saved: but hope that is seen is not hope: for who hopeth for that which he seeth? But if we hope for that which we see not, then do we with patience wait for it. And in like manner also the Spirit helpeth our infirmity: for we know not how to pray as we ought; but the Spirit himself maketh intercession for us with groanings which cannot be uttered; and he that searcheth the hearts knoweth what is the mind of the Spirit, because he maketh intercession for the saints according to the will of God.

Now the God of peace, who brought again from the dead the great shepherd of the sheep with the blood of the eternal covenant, even our Lord Jesus, make you perfect in every good thing to do his will, working in us that which is well-pleasing in his sight, through Jesus Christ; to whom be the glory for ever and ever. Amen.

7

PRAYER AND SACRAMENTS

THIS evening our subject is 'Prayer and Sacraments.'
But I only mean to speak of one Sacrament—the Holy
Communion. The aim of all prayer is the same as the
aim of all life, it is union with God. Life and prayer
should be as closely as possible intertwined. God is the
ultimate reality who sustains all existence, including our
own lives. To be in actual and living union with Him
is the fundamental business of life; and everything else
follows from that.

He has given us our duty in the world to do, and it
is our duty to Him to perform it as thoroughly and
effectively as possible. We shall do it best if, while we
are engaged in the tasks He has given us, we give them
our whole and complete attention; therefore, during that
time, we cannot be specifically and directly thinking
about Him. But, of course, we shall enter upon those
tasks with minds perpetually refreshed by the memory
of Him and of His love, and it is most desirable that
not only on Sundays, nor only at regular times of prayer,
but also at any moments when our attention is not
definitely claimed by the work we have in hand, our
minds should go back to God as He is in Himself; and
we shall thus be constantly remembering Him. There
ought to be no sense of spiritual transition as we pass
from any occupation which is our proper occupation

at the time to the thought of God. We should feel, whether it be in performing the duty He has given us or in remembering Him who gave us the duty, that we are always seeking to deepen our union with Him. But the moments when we concentrate upon this purpose particularly are our times of prayer.

Let us be quite clear about what are not the aims of prayer. We are not, in our prayers, trying to suggest to God something He has not thought of. That would plainly be ridiculous. Nor are we trying to change His mind. That would be an enterprise blasphemous in the attempt, and calamitous in the accomplishment. He knows what we want before we ask it. Then why ask? Why, because there may be blessings which only are effectively blessings to those who are in the right condition of mind; just as there is wholesome food which is actually wholesome only to those who are healthy in body. If you give the best beef to somebody in typhoid fever, you do him great harm. The worst of all diseases of the soul is forgetfulness of God; and if everything that we need came to us while we forgot God, we should only be confirmed in our forgetfulness of Him, in our sense of independence of Him. It may be good for a man that a temptation which always beats him should continue, and continue to defeat him, rather than he should conquer it without knowing that the power in which he won his conquest was from God. So, over and over again, it will happen that, whether or not God can give the blessing which, in His love, He desires to give, will depend on whether or not we recognise the source from which it comes. The way to recognise that

He is the source of the blessings, and that we need them, is to ask. This expresses our sense of dependence upon God for that blessing. And remember that the only object of using words in your prayers is to fix your own thoughts, not to give information to God. He can read your thoughts, but your thoughts are likely to be very vague and wandering unless you fix them by means of words. It is for your own sake, not for God's, that you put your prayers into words. That being so, in your private prayers, those are the right words which succeed in fixing your thoughts on the right objects. It does not matter whether they would assist anybody else to fix their thoughts there or not; it would not matter if you invented an entirely new language of your own for your prayers. The words that help you are the right words for you to use.

When we come to public worship, it is different. Here the worship gathers us together in a common aspiration and a common sense of dependence upon God. Here, then, the language should be the most beautiful we can find for the purpose, suggesting in its beauty the reverence we owe to the Divine Majesty. Moreover, it should very often express not only the things we do feel, but the things we ought to feel, so that we may, by our prayer, teach ourselves to feel those things more thoroughly than we have done.

But the aim is union with God, not changing His mind, but changing our own, in order that, as a result of our faith, our realisation that we depend upon Him, He may be able to do for us, or through us, what, until we are conscious of this, He cannot do. The proper outline of a Christian prayer is not 'Please do for me what I want.' It is 'Please do with me what You want.' That prayer will always be answered in proportion to its sincerity.

And in order that it may be prayer at all, it must be addressed to God. Those of us who try to say our prayers nearly all find times when they are very cold and dry. There are many reasons for this, but one of the commonest reasons is we have let ourselves slip into forgetting God even while we pray. We use His Name but do not stop to think what it means. Our minds are focused on the things we ask for, and not upon God. That is not praying; that is uttering wishes to no one in particular. I cannot imagine anything more tedious or more futile. Naturally, people who get fixed in that habit say they find their prayers are no good, so they give them up. What they were doing was no good; but it was not praying.

Praying is speaking to God; so the first necessity is that you should be directing your mind towards God. That is the best part and most important part of prayer anyhow, and without it all the rest is useless. The great aim is union with God, and the first need is that you should be, so far as you are capable, with open face gazing upon Him. And then, when you have remembered what you know about God (which is not difficult, because He has given us the portrait of Himself in Jesus Christ, and though you cannot see God you can always remember Jesus Christ; so you should never begin to pray until you have the figure of Christ before your mind, and should pray to God as you see Him there);

then you turn to the things you will pray for, and this is to be after the manner of the Lord's Prayer. I wonder where most of you begin to mean business as you say the Lord's Prayer. I used often to ask that of boys at school when I was preparing them for Confirmation. Their answer, when they gave any, was always the same: 'Forgive us our trespasses'; but that is rather near the end. The reason, of course, was that this was the first thing they knew they wanted and knew they could only get from God. If they had been both hungry and hard up, I suppose they would have started with 'daily bread.' But our Lord says that when you come into the presence of God you should forget all about yourself and your needs, even your sins; you should be so filled with the thought of God that what you want above all things is that God's Name may be hallowed—reverenced— throughout the world. You are to ask for that first, because you ought to want it most. And next, that He may be effectively King of the world He has made, so that all men obey His law; and then, that His whole purpose of love shall be carried out unspoiled by the selfishness of men. We have got into a habit of saying, 'God's will be done,' in a mood of resignation. That is blasphemous. It means that, having found we cannot have our own way, we are ready to put up with His as a second best. It will not do. We ought to say, 'Thy Will be done,' in ungovernable hope, knowing it to be so much better than our own. Then you ask for freedom from anxiety, 'daily bread,' to see your way one day ahead; that is little enough. Then, for the sense of His favour, without which you cannot serve Him with a full

heart, and which you have so often forfeited; you must
be forgiven if you are to serve him whole-heartedly.
Then that there may be no unnecessary difficulties, 'Lead
us not into temptation.' And there is some evil that has
actually got hold of us now, we want deliverance from
that. And all this is not because then we shall be good
and happy, but because it is God's kingdom, power,
and glory we are concerned about all the time.

It is the prayer you would want to offer if you loved
God with all your heart and you may learn to love Him
with all your heart if you realise what this prayer means,
and try to enter into it. Never let it become for you a
mere formula.

In our Lord's teaching about petitionary prayer there
are three main principles. The first is confidence, the
second is perseverance and the third, for lack of a better
word, I will call correspondence with Christ. Confidence:
you remember He used language so strong as to be
almost violent about the confidence with which you are
to pray. If only you believe you have the thing, if it is
moving a mountain into the sea, you shall have it. He
never took any pains to avoid being misunderstood. He
wanted people to think out for themselves the application
of the principles He gave; so He added no qualifications.
But He went straight on apparently to something else
which seems inconsistent: perseverance. When you pray,
you are to be sure you will get the thing; and if you do
not get it, you are to go on praying. He illustrates it by
the parable of the unjust judge, who ultimately granted
the woman's petition because she was becoming such
a nuisance. This, of course, is one of those parables

which derive part of their point from the fact that the suggested illustration will not work. We know that God does not grant our petitions to rid Himself of tedium at our persistence; and, amongst other things, our Lord is here saying that if you will think of God as first and foremost a Judge you will find Him a curious kind of Judge. He does indeed judge us. But He is not first Judge —He is first Father, and only judges as a father judges.

There is nothing that so much develops faith as to persevere in asking through disappointment. If you always get the blessing you seek at once, or something you recognise as corresponding to it, your faith will remain at about the level at which you started. The reason why God calls for perseverance is not, of course, that He wishes to test our faith. He knows exactly what it is worth. But He may wish to deepen it. The thing that will most deepen it is to persist with faith through disappointment. Many masters of the spiritual life have said it seemed to them, as a matter of experience, that at an early stage in the spiritual life God does answer some prayers quite directly, and then begins to stop. The next stage is one in which prayers do not often receive a perceptible answer. God always does answer prayer; He always acts in response to prayer; but often we cannot understand His actions. Your confidence in praying ought not to be chiefly confidence that you are going to get what you ask, because that will be confidence as much in your own judgement as in God. It has to be a real surrender to Him. You must pass from faith that God will give you what you ask, to faith that what He gives is better than what you asked.

Now these two first principles of confidence and perseverance our Lord gave in His public teaching; but to the disciples alone He added that the prayer always answered was the prayer that was offered in His Name. 'Hitherto,' He said, 'have ye asked nothing in My Name. Ask and ye shall receive.' What does asking in anyone's name mean? It does not mean only tacking on the words, 'Through Jesus Christ our Lord.' As Studdert Kennedy used to say, it does not mean that our Lord has signed a large number of blank cheques on the bank of heaven, and you can fill them in how you like. To act in anyone's name is to act as his representative. To pray in the name of Christ is to pray as He would pray—as He is praying now. He is first and foremost the great illustration of perfect submission to the Will of God. So we are led on to understand that, as the great purpose of prayer is union with God, so the thing we are to express in our prayer is complete submission to His will that He may do it for us, in us, through us.

The two sons of Zebedee once came to our Lord and started off with a quite exact illustration of the wrong way to pray: 'We would that Thou shouldest do for us whatsoever we shall ask of Thee.' He asks what it is; and it turns out to be something that is selfish in the radically bad sense; it is something from which, if they obtain it, other people are shut out; it is to sit on His right and left hand in His glory. Then comes the answer: 'Can you drink of the cup that I drink of and be baptised with the baptism I am baptised with?' They would have something for themselves; He asks whether they can share His sacrifice. Incidentally, He thus suggests to them what is the nature of that glory which they seek conspicuously to share. But that is not our main concern just now. God answers every prayer; but when you come praying after the formula, 'We would Thou shouldest do for us whatsoever we shall ask of Thee,' there is only one answer you will get: 'Can you share my sacrifice?' If your prayer is selfish, the answer will be something that will rebuke your selfishness. You may not recognise it as having come at all, but it is sure to be there.

So all prayer, and the life of which it is the focusing point, becomes that offering of ourselves in union with the sacrifice of Christ, which finds its perfect expression in the Eucharist.

There are very many ways in which we may approach the consideration of the Holy Communion. I say that because I shall, of course, be able to adopt only one. You must not suppose that, if the way in which I approach it does not help to make it more real to you, there is no other way of approach by which you might find it real and ever more real.

We traced one day during the week the outline of our Lord's Ministry, and on Thursday evening, in very sketchy outline, we considered the stages by which He challenged the authority of the High Priests and made it inevitable that they should either accept Him as the promised Messiah or pronounce Him a blasphemer, with the condemnation to death that would follow. After His conduct in the triumphal entry, and cleansing of the Temple, there was no avoidance of that choice.

During the last week, with the same careful pains with which He arranged for the triumphal entry, we find also He has arranged for His Last Supper. As you know, the New Testament contains accounts based apparently upon different chronologies, and there is some doubt whether the Last Supper was the Passover Feast or not. It seems likely at least that St John is right in maintaining that it took place, not on the proper day of the Passover meal, but the day before. It is agreed that the day of the feast that year fell on a Sabbath, and it would have been lawful and probable that the Passover feast had been transferred a day earlier. So it may have been the actual Paschal meal, though not on the actual day of the feast. This is comparatively of small moment.

His disciples ask what preparations they are to make. He tells them to go to the city and they will meet a man carrying a pitcher of water. Women as a rule carried water, so they would not make a mistake. He would say nothing, but would turn and walk to the appointed place, and they were to follow him. When they came there, they were to speak the password just as when they went to fetch the ass on which He would ride; they were to say, 'Where is My guest chamber, where I shall eat the Passover with My disciples,' and he would show them the Upper Room furnished for them. Why are the directions given in this curious cypher? Surely the reason is evident; Judas must not know. He must not be able to bring the soldiers there. It would have been the easiest place to effect the arrest if only he had known for certain where the Lord would be; and there must be no interruption there.

The Lord has lived the perfect life of perfect love. In the threefold temptations He has repudiated the method of obtaining men's allegiance otherwise than by the free offering of love; and now there is one of His own friends who is meditating treachery. What shall He do? What took place in the Upper Room was the spiritual crisis of the whole ministry. It would have been the easiest thing in the world to give the order to Peter, and the rest, and have the traitor bound. So the Lord would have made His escape; and so He would have lost His Kingdom. He tells them, and in telling them, shows Judas that He knows his mind, and therefore ensures that what He is about to do shall not be misunderstood by him— He tells them that one of them shall betray Him; and the beloved disciple, leaning back on His breast, asks: 'Who is it?' and into his ear the secret is whispered. 'He it is to whom I shall give the first sop when I have dipped it.' He singles Judas out for special honour. He makes to him, without giving away his secret to the rest, the one appeal that love still can make, and watches the effect. St John, who knows the secret, watches also; and what he saw stands written. 'After the sop, then entered Satan into him.' He has seen the man's face go black; the Lord, too, has seen it. 'That thou doest, do quickly,' and Judas passes out under his Lord's protecting silence. That was the great spiritual crisis: that was the moment when He had to determine whether He should be loyal to the whole principle on which He came to found His Kingdom, even though it must mean that nothing now could stop the arrest, trial and crucifixion. 'He then having received the sop, went immediately out; and it was night'—a glimpse, through the door of the lighted room, of the darkness into which the traitor went. And then the Lord did two things. First, He said, 'Now is the Son of Man glorified.' Whether they were the authentic words or St John's understanding of His mind it does not matter. We shall not get a better understanding of His mind than that reached by the writer of the Fourth Gospel. That was the moment when the Son of Man achieved His glory. When it was so easy and so innocent to desert the principle of His Kingdom and save Himself from all the anguish, He was loyal to the cause for which He came; and the Cross after this was, from one point of view, a mere consequence.

In that moment also He took the bread that was before Him; and said it was His Body; and broke it. For in that moment He had broken His Body, and in that moment He had offered His side to the soldier's spear. 'This is My Body.' What would they think? Remember this was late on Thursday evening; by nine o'clock on Friday morning He was on the Cross. As they looked back, the two things would seem very close together, and they would know that one thing at least that He meant was this: As I break this bread, so I am breaking My Body. But not vainly; I am breaking it to give it to you, that the sacrifice of which it is the vehicle may enter into you and be your own. In the Consecration Prayer the words are there: 'In the same night that He was betrayed.' What we do when we come to the Holy Communion is, among other things, at least also this, that we unite ourselves with the thing He did that night in the supreme spiritual crisis of His ministry in order that the meaning of what He did may become true of us as it was of Him—that His sacrifice may be ours.

How are we to think of the way in which He still offers Himself to us by this means? There is no complete analogy, but there are some that are not very remote. When you listen to beautiful music, where is the beauty? You do not create it: you do not invent it—you find it. And yet you will not find it unless you have the understanding of music which qualifies you to be sensitive to it. It is the same with beauty everywhere. Two men stand before some great picture. Both see the same colours and the same lines—one sees beauty, the other sees nothing significant. But the one who sees the beauty does not make it—the artist made it. And so in the Holy Communion Christ offers Himself in all His fullness of holiness and love to be ours, but whether you receive Him depends on the insight of your faith, on how far you are conscious of your need of Him, on how far you are sincere in seeking to be united with Him in His offering of Himself to the Father.

At least a great part of what is cared for by those who speak of the Real Presence is this, that Christ there offers Himself in the fullness of His self-sacrifice to you that you may receive Him; and the chief part of what those care about who dwell especially on His Presence in the faithful receiver, is that unless you come in the mind to be united to Him so far as you may, you will not receive Him. For it is a law of the spiritual life from which there is no escape, that we receive in propor-

tion to what we give—much more than we give, thank
God, or we should be in a sorry plight, but still in
proportion.

If you come there giving nothing, with no intention
that your life should be used by God and for Him, then
you will receive nothing. He will be offering you His
perfect life of love, but you will be shutting it out. When
you come with those things about you which are the
opposite of God, because they are the opposite of love
—envy, contempt, resentment, spite—they make a block,
in the channel through which the life of Christ might
reach you. And all of us are selfish, more or less; and
none can perfectly receive that perfect gift. So we need
to come there offering ourselves in His service, and seek
to receive out of the gift which He offers in its completeness and perfection so much as we are able to
receive, and then go out into the world to live by that,
a little more loving, a little less selfish; then back again,
able this time, because a little more loving and a little
less selfish, to receive rather more fully that always
perfect gift; until life and worship build one another
up into a complete dedication, and you give yourself
utterly to His service, and you not only aspire to mean
but you do actually mean the words of the great prayer,
'Here we offer and present unto Thee, O Lord, ourselves,
our souls and bodies, to be a reasonable, holy, and
lively sacrifice unto Thee.' When you can say that, with
nothing held back and with nothing forgotten, then you
will receive the gift of the life of Christ in all its fullness,
and will say with St Paul, 'I live, yet not I, but Christ
liveth in me.' Until we can say that, and say it truly,

we must no one of us be content. And there is no means by which we may so fully enter into the meaning of His Sacrifice as this which He has provided and which is adapted to our whole nature. For we are called upon to use our bodies as well as our spirits in the act by which we seek to receive the life of Christ to be our own, since while we are in the body our service will be unreal unless our bodies are given to it. And we recognise His gift for what it is, the life that is offered in sacrifice to God, wholly given to Him to be used by Him not for our purpose but for His.

For I received of the Lord that which also I delivered unto you, how that the Lord Jesus in the night in which he was betrayed took bread; and when he had given thanks, he brake it, and said, This is my body which is for you: this do in remembrance of me. In like manner also the cup, after supper, saying, This cup is the new covenant in my blood: this do, as oft as ye drink it, in remembrance of me. For as often as ye eat this bread, and drink the cup, ye proclaim the Lord's death till he come.

I am the true vine, and my Father is the husbandman. Every branch in me that beareth not fruit, he taketh it away: and every branch that beareth fruit, he cleanseth it, that it may bear more fruit. Already ye are clean because of the word which I have spoken unto you. Abide in me, and I in you. As the branch cannot bear fruit of itself, except it abide in the vine; so neither can ye, except ye abide in me. I am the vine, ye are the branches: he that abideth in me, and I in him, the same beareth much fruit: for apart from me ye can do nothing. If a man abide not in me, he is cast forth as a branch, and is withered; and they gather them, and cast them into the fire, and they are burned. If ye abide in me, and my words in you, ask whatsoever ye will, and it shall be done unto you. Herein is my Father glorified, that ye bear much fruit; and so shall ye be my disciples. Even as the Father has loved me, I also have loved you: abide ye in my love.

And the God of peace himself sanctify you wholly; and may your spirit and soul and body be preserved entire, without blame at the coming of our Lord Jesus Christ.

8

THE CHRISTIAN SOCIETY

DURING this week we have been trying, so far as the time and limitations of capacity—yours and mine—might allow, to consider the character of God and His purpose for the world (for it is nothing less than that), and His purpose for us as the part of His purpose for the world with which each one of us is directly and immediately concerned. And it is always in that context that we ought to think of the life of Christ and of our duty in response to the call of Christ. If we think of it against a narrower background we may easily devote ourselves with enthusiasm to some course which, though effective in itself, is yet far less effective in the long run —which is, in the end, the only run that matters—than it might have been had we kept before us the true perspective in which God's revelation is always set throughout the Bible. If you have doubt whether that is indeed the right way for us to regard the life of Christ and His call upon us, then I ask you to read again the first chapter of St Paul's Epistle to the Ephesians. He sets forth the eternal purpose of God for which He made the world, as being to 'sum up all things in Christ.'

And, in the long course of that purpose's fulfilment, we have considered the supreme and crucial moment, the life and the death of Jesus Christ, and the new impulse which came into the world as a result of that revelation—the new power over the hearts of men which they found that God was exercising, and to which they gave the name Holy Spirit, afterwards reading back what they had learned through that experience into all other activities of God at work within nature and within mankind in fulfilment of His own eternal purpose and in response to the manifestation of His character. We have seen that the purpose of the life of our Lord was quite definitely the inauguration of the Kingdom of God, the rule of God in the world, but therein also the revelation of God who is King—a revelation which designates Him as perfect love, so that we may paraphrase the description of His purpose by saying it is the inauguration of the reign of love.

When His visible Presence was withdrawn from men's sight, what was left as the fruit of His Ministry? Not a formulated creed, not a body of writings in which a new philosophy of life was expounded, but a group of men and women who found themselves knit together in a fellowship closer than any that they had known, and who became the nucleus of the whole Christian Church. As the fellowship expanded, it drew within its bounds people of every type, every nation, every social class. And they found that so far as they were loyal to its inner purpose, and submitted themselves to that Spirit moving in it by which its life was constituted, all that separated them from one another became unimportant and negligible. There was neither Jew nor Gentile—the deepest of all divisions based on religious history, negligible; neither Greek nor barbarian—the deepest of all divisions based on education and culture, negligible; neither bond nor free—the deepest of all divisions in economic status, negligible; neither male nor female—even the distinction of sex on which the whole social fabric rests, negligible. The whole group of them constituted a single personality, because all governed by one spirit and purpose, and the centre of unity in any personality is its purpose. And St Paul sees that 'one man in Christ Jesus' growing from strength to strength as new races bring in their various talents and endowments, until all come to constitute the 'one man in Christ Jesus' full-grown; and that is the measure of the stature of the completeness of the Christ. For we shall never know what Christ is in the fullness of His power until He has all nations at His disposal to manifest through their peculiar gifts the various elements in His all-embracing purpose.

The name of this fellowship, which ought ideally to be so close as to constitute a single personality, is the Church. St Paul speaks of the Church as the Body of Christ, and what He means first and foremost by that is, of course, that as Jesus of Nazareth used the body of flesh and blood in order to live before men the life which interprets to them the very being of God, so the Church exists on earth to do the self-same thing. It is the means whereby Christ becomes active and carries out His purpose in the world; that is what it is for, and that is what makes it the Church—the life of His Spirit within it, rising out of its faith in Him. And that remains true of it even when the people who are the members of the Church from time to time become very feeble in their faith, so that the activity of His Spirit by means of them is very much hampered and limited. No doubt, as we look upon the actual Christian Church at many periods of history, including our own, we may find that in many respects it presents an uninspiring spectacle. That is because we are attending to things which are incidental, rather than to the things that make it the Church of Christ, His Body. Those things are the perpetual witness of the Gospel in its reading and its proclamation, the perpetual ministry of its sacraments, and supremely the Sacrament of the Holy Communion, of which we were speaking yesterday, where we do again the thing that Christ did at the supreme crisis of His Ministry in order that by imitation of His outward act we may be united in His spiritual self-giving. In the book of the Revelation, there is a vision of the Word of God going forth conquering and to conquer, and of the armies in heaven following Him. That is the true picture of the Church. And we have to remember that many of the fruits of the Church's existence and activity are to be found entirely outside its own specific organisation; for wherever you find the Spirit of Christ gaining hold among men, there you see the result of the continual activity of the Church across the ages.

Over and over again, no doubt, it may happen that there arises a group of people who think they can serve God very much better independently of this ecclesiastical organisation. Where did they learn about Christ? If there had been no organisation the knowledge of Him would never have reached them. When we take the long view, which we must take if we are thinking of God's eternal purpose to sum up all things in Christ, we recognise at once that organisation is completely and absolutely necessary, and our duty is not to cut ourselves loose from it, but to try to share the life which it exists to foster. And it is certainly true that no man can be a good Christian by himself. No man is able to understand more than a tiny fraction of the unsearchable riches of Christ; he needs the supplementing contribution of his neighbour's apprehension. And as it is true that no individual alone can be a really good Christian, so it is true that the full Christian life cannot be lived only in groups of like-minded Christians; for if they are like-minded they merely strengthen one another in those elements of Christian faith and experience in which they are already fairly strong. That is good as far as it goes, and these associations have their perfectly real place, for they generate a degree of enthusiasm and zeal which it is perhaps impossible to produce in the wider fellow-ship of the Church if it has no such lesser fellowships within it. But if such associations keep themselves apart from, and do not freely mingle with, other associations of people whose apprehension of Christ has been other than their own, they tend to stereotype their limitations as well as strengthen their faith, and in the end they may easily become causes of division, which weaken the whole Church in its witness, and so may even do harm as great as the good they do. It must be in the widest fellowship we can find, and a fellowship that bears the promise of permanence from age to age, that we are to fulfil the obligations of our membership.

As Christ's purpose was to found a Kingdom, so we should think of the Church as the army of that Kingdom. It is, no doubt, true that we have repeatedly substituted compromise for warfare and prudence for the spirit of adventure. The world in which the Church is set to work has, over and over again, made terms with it, which the Church of that period has most wrongly accepted. One of the commonest of the compromises that have been made is for the world to allow the Church to be at peace in proclaiming what may be called its philosophical paradoxes provided that it keeps quiet about its moral ones. And to some extent we have to confess that the Church, as we ourselves constitute it, has fallen into the snare. We have shown, no doubt, a disproportion of concern about the distinctive philosophical doctrines of Christianity as compared with the moral duties of all disciples of Christ. We have, for example, been much more silent than we ought concerning Christ's perfectly plain teaching on the subject of wealth and poverty. We have not driven home upon men His clear intuition that though, if wealth comes, it ought to be accepted and used as an opportunity, yet it must be recognised as rather a snare to the spiritual life than an aim which the Christian may legitimately set before himself to pursue. The ways in which this compromise has been effected have varied of course from one generation to another. The vital matter is that we in our time should try to be honest with ourselves about it. Inevitably, during this week we have been trying to see the Christian Faith, first and foremost so far as we may, as truth. Tonight we have got to see it, as far as we may, as duty. When you come to the thought of the society which Christ has placed in the world to represent Him, you are confronted with the challenge of Christian duty. If it seems to you that the Church as organised has somehow lost sense of proportion, remember that only through the Church has the Gospel ever reached you, and that only through the Church can it reach the ages far ahead. And you will do more service to the cause of Christ by bringing what reality you can into its life than you can ever render by staying outside and doing what seems possible to you, or you and your few friends, in isolation.

But the way in which we are to think of this society must never be primarily in relation to itself. An army does not exist for its own benefit; it exists for its kingdom and its king; and you must come to the Church not chiefly for what you can gain from it, but for what you can give to it. When you come like that, you will gain far more than if you come looking for gain. If you ever catch yourself saying, 'I got no good from it, so I gave up going,' remember that only proves you were coming in the frame of mind in which you were not likely to get much good. Come to lend yourself as a member of the Body of Christ—one of His limbs, to be moved according to His will in co-operation with all the other limbs in His Body. That is the claim. And the issue that depends on the vitality of the Church, which you by your decision may a good deal affect, is at any given moment the great question of human history.

For in the last resort there are only two pivots about which human life can revolve, and we are always organising society and ourselves about one or other of them. They are self and God. In the great book with which the Bible closes, these two principles are set before us under the symbolic figures of the 'Lamb standing, as it had been slain'—the symbol of love that uses sacrifice as its instrument—and the great wild beast, the symbol of self-will or pride, whose instrument is force. And they work out into two civilisations. The principle of self and pride can only build up Babylon the Great, and Babylon the Great always comes tumbling down again. But by the activity among men of the principle of love, which must always show itself in sacrifice, there is built among men the heavenly City, the New Jerusalem which comes down, whensoever it comes, and in whatsoever degree it comes, out of Heaven from God. In every generation, but in a very peculiar sense in ours, the question has to be answered, What is to be built? There have been few moments in the history of mankind when the issue has been so naked as it is in ours. Which city is to be built? Babylon the Great, which has tumbled down so often, and will always tumble down again, or the City which you cannot build yourselves, but which God can build through you, if unitedly you give yourselves to be used by Him as its builders? And the body that must answer this question is always the Church. No individuals can answer it; it must be the whole fellowship of Christ's disciples. And you can help towards the right answer just in the degree in which you associate yourself with it in its age-long effort.

And, remember, the supreme wonder of the history of the Christian Church is that always in the moments when it has seemed most dead, out of its own body there has sprung up new life; so that in age after age it has renewed itself, and age after age by its renewal has carried the world forward into new stages of progress, as it will do for us in our day, if only we give ourselves in devotion to its Lord and take our place in its service.

Now we come to the question, What are you going to do? You will feel quite rightly that what I am able to suggest is thoroughly pedestrian, and that is part of the test of our sincerity. It is rather agreeable than otherwise to expand the mind by the contemplation of an eternal purpose, and there is perhaps a certain amount of thrill and glamour about the conception of the age-long purpose of God now to be wrought out through His Church. But when we come to what we can do ourselves, it always seems so little, as, of course, it is. What each one alone can do is always very little, but the way great things are done is by all doing that very little unitedly. And it is the test of our sincerity whether we are ready to do the little things that are in our power —the things that have not about them a great thrill and glamour, the things that are rather dull, the things that we can only do, if we do them at all, because we are genuinely loyal and because we have a purpose that is firmly set, because we have a firm determination to serve Christ as we have the opportunity. Remember that the test which is coming to each one of you of the value which this week has been to you, is going to be found almost entirely in relation to quite small things, the multitude of which will carry their great weight in swaying the balance this way or that for the life of Oxford in the days that are coming.

While it is true that what each of you does is small,

will you at least make up your minds whether all that
you have been thinking of this week is genuinely your
concern? The pressure of practical affairs in life is very
great. If we are conscientiously to do the duty that lies
before us, it often seems that it will claim nearly all our
energy. Is it not enough that each man should do his
own job thoroughly and conscientiously, and leave all
this speculation (as he will call it if he is in the mood
to talk like this at all) concerning the purpose of God
for the world to other people who are interested in such
things, and perhaps especially to those who may be regarded as being personally committed to that aspect of
life, which means the clergy? But, is it not plainly true
that the real value of your job depends upon the truth,
speaking broadly at least, of those things of which we
have been thinking this week? Is there not a grave
possibility, if you leave that out of sight, that you are
committing yourself to futility? Is it not certain that any
man will do the job allotted to him with more understanding, and therefore more efficiently, if he understands
a little the place which it takes in the general development of human welfare? And if it is true that God, the
Almighty and Eternal, is watching over each one of us
with the love that we see in Jesus Christ, is it, then,
conceivable that it is not the concern of each one that
he should know that love and consider what it means
to him and for him? Will you first, then, genuinely think
again, is it your concern? Can you even dare to say
'No' to that? And if it is, then the duty follows to reach
a decision—not necessarily now, not necessarily this
next week, but to reach a decision in time to be effective

in your life. And you must realise that the greatest decisions always have to be taken before there is a complete sufficiency of evidence, because it is only after they have been made, and the experiment tried out, that the evidence can be there.

So when you have decided, as I urge you must decide, that this is your concern, your own individual concern, then what decision are you going to make about it? Are you going to hear and heed the call of Christ or not? And again, when you have answered, as you must, that you cannot set it on one side, there follows inevitably the duty of making Him known to your neighbours. The ways in which this may be done are infinitely various, but the duty is absolute and constant. His gift of Himself, that is to say of perfect love, is not something which you can have and keep. If you are keeping it, it proves you have not got it. Every Christian is a missionary, and if he is not a missionary he is not yet truly or deeply a Christian at all. He may be seeking to become one; but he is not yet one who has received the love of Christ in his soul; because that love is of such a kind that, wherever it is, it must go on to give itself to others.

We are most of us very shy about speaking of spiritual things. That has its root partly in real reverence; we do not wish to speak too easily or too unworthily about those things which we realise as greatest. And yet where people are on fire with any kind of zeal they can hardly keep themselves from some kind of speech, and most of us ought to conquer some part of our shyness and be ready to speak at the appropriate time. But at least all Christians have got to aim at being such people that our friends see in us a kind of life they would like to live and of which they want to know the secret. You have got to exhibit the winsome attractiveness of Christ. Individually, then, we must consider, is it my concern? Yes. Can I refuse its call? Assuredly not. If I obey then I am committed to making known what has come to me.

Now let us turn to more immediate action that you can take. First, let us gather in great numbers tomorrow at the Holy Communion to offer thanks for what God has done for us this week. We do not know what it is. Nobody knows what the upshot of this week is going to be, and nobody can know. But it is not conceivable that there should have been so many of you gathered here day by day to spend a little time at least in realising the meaning of Christ, and joining in prayer to God through Him, without result. What it will be we do not know; but let us give thanks at least that God did gather us together and make the opportunity for us, and let us dedicate ourselves in His service that that opportunity may be used. Then try to recall some parts at least of what you have heard this week. Think it over and decide how far you can accept it. I hope there will be groups in colleges and other places to discuss these subjects. The way you may most easily open your minds to receive the truth of God more fully is to see how far you agree with what has been put before you and to make that much your own. Then I would especially urge that you should consider together the use that might be made of that wonderful endowment which we have in Oxford for the furtherance of its spiritual life, in the college chapels—both by attendance at services now being held, and through thinking out what would meet your need in some other way, and consulting with the chaplain of the college how that may be done.

Take the opportunities that come. I would plead that whatever is done as a direct continuation of this Mission should be kept as wide at least as the Church of England. It is right that there should be other associations representing special points of view and the determination to follow special kinds of Christian activity, because in them men generate a keener enthusiasm; but let them not be separated from the whole wide fellowship in which we strengthen and enrich one another.

It is inevitable that the suggestions made should seem pedestrian and small; only remember that your first duty while you are here is preparation for the life that is to come. Your first duty is not forthwith to be rendering in full form the kind of service to which your life is to be given, but to make yourself ready for that service when the time comes so that it may be as effective as it can. Because that is your duty, therefore the opportunities for these more specific forms of Christian service must be comparatively limited. But you are preparing for a life which you mean to live for Christ. You must look forward to it as this, and seek to do the will of God in and by your work. Never imagine that vocation is to the ministry alone. Every man has his own vocation, and must try to find it. The work which has now to be done for God in the world is not work for the clergy alone; it is the work of the whole Church, the whole body of the disciples of Christ, in which every man must be finding God's will for him, and doing that.

But if you are in doubt how you may best lay out your life, and if you are quite clear in your acceptance of Jesus Christ as your Saviour and your God, then the mere circumstances of the time constitute a call to the Church's direct service in its ministry which you must face; for there is no sphere of life in which a man can more certainly lay out all his talents in the service of God. It will call for every capacity; it will bring you into touch with human beings in every conceivable relation. There is no life so rich or so full of all those joys which come from serving people at the point of their greatest need. But these things are for you to think over. What is clear is that the King is calling, and you must answer. He calls not to comfort nor to power, as the world reckons power; He calls for heroic service. Has it occurred to you that you will search the Gospels in vain for such words as these: 'If any man will come after Me, I will deliver him from the pains of hell and give him the joys of Heaven.' It would have been quite true; but He did not say it. He did, indeed, say: 'Come unto Me all ye that labour and are heavy laden, and I will give you rest.' And if you are weighed down under the burden of the evil in your own soul and in the world, that invitation is addressed to you. But that is not the nature of His appeal for followers. That appeal is to deny yourself and take up your cross and follow Him. It is the appeal of the heroes of all ages.

You know how Garibaldi saved the Roman republic in spirit, though its body perished. The little state that had been founded in Rome was falling before the combined assault of the corrupt states round about it. The siege had lasted for more weeks than the experts thought it could last days, but at last the day of surrender had come, and into the great concourse of citizens there rode the man whose faith and heroism had sustained it all the while. He said, 'I am going out from Rome. I offer neither quarters, nor provisions, nor wages; I offer hunger, thirst, forced marches, battles, death. Let him who loves his country with his heart and not with his lips only, follow me.' And they streamed out after him into the hills, and because of his heroism and theirs, there is a kingdom of Italy today. It was a paraphrase of the appeal of Christ. 'I offer neither quarters, nor provisions, nor wages'; 'if any man will come after Me, let him forget about himself and be ready for whatever it involves, and follow Me.' And if we would stream out after Him, there might be a Kingdom of God in Oxford tomorrow.

The King is calling, and you must answer; for to give no answer is to answer 'No.' That is the thought I want to leave with you. You have heard—however poorly expressed—His call: and you must answer, because to give no answer is to answer 'No.'

But you will answer 'Yes,' and so take your place in the great fellowship of worship and of service, the eternal Church, the communion of saints, the army in heaven which rides in the train of the Word of God as He goes forth conquering and to conquer.

O Lord Jesu Christ, Thou Word and Revelation of the Eternal Father, come, we beseech Thee, and take possession of our souls. So fill our minds with the thought and our imaginations with the picture of Thy love, that there may be in us no room for any thought or desire that is discordant with Thy holy will. Cleanse us, we pray Thee, of all that may make us deaf to Thy call or slow to obey it, who with the Father and the Holy Ghost art one God, blessed for evermore. Amen.

May the love of the Lord Jesus draw you to Himself;
May the power of the Lord Jesus strengthen you in His service;
May the joy of the Lord Jesus fill your souls; and
May the blessing of God Almighty, the Father, the Son, and the Holy Ghost, be upon you and remain with you always.